A Drama of the Southwest

A Drama of the Southwest

The Critical Edition of a Forgotten Play by

JEAN TOOMER

edited by CAROLYN J. DEKKER

UNIVERSITY OF NEW MEXICO PRESS | ALBUQUERQUE

Printed in the United States of America

First paperback edition, 2026
Paperback ISBN: 978-0-8263-7044-0

Library of Congress Cataloging-in-Publication Data

Toomer, Jean, 1894–1967.
A drama of the Southwest : the critical edition of a forgotten play / Jean Toomer ; edited by Carolyn J. Dekker.
pages cm
Includes bibliographical references and index.
ISBN 978-0-8263-5638-3 (cloth : alk. paper) — ISBN 978-0-8263-5639-0 (electronic)
I. Dekker, Carolyn J., 1983– editor. II. Title.
PS3539.O478D73 2016
812'.52—dc23

2015018008

Cover photograph: © Wick Beavers, *San Francisco de Assisi with snow and pigeons Rancho de Taos*
Designed by Lisa Tremaine
Composed in Joanna MT

Contents

Preface

More than nine decades after the publication of *Cane*, I am proud to present *A Drama of the Southwest*, a previously unseen work by Jean Toomer. I hope it will be of interest to, perhaps even precious to, devoted readers of Toomer and the many poets and writers working today for whom *Cane* has been a beacon.

The introduction and notes in this edition are intended to make it more accessible to scholars of African American literature or American modernist writing who may be familiar with Toomer but not with Taos and its artist colony in the early twentieth century, as well as for scholars who may be familiar with that southwestern scene but not with Toomer and his place within it.

Many scholars of Toomer know *A Drama of the Southwest* already by reputation, and perhaps not favorably: it is reputed to be inconclusive, didactic, or failed. This edition recovers the play by providing a wholly new text, a hybrid of two surviving but partial drafts. These consist of the typed draft of four scenes (scenes 1–4 in this edition) that has thus far monopolized scholarly attention, and a much larger handwritten manuscript (scenes 5–13). In seeking to disrupt narratives of Toomer's late-career failure, my scholarly and editorial approach has been this: Read Toomer. Read all there is of him. By releasing *A Drama of the Southwest* from the archive and into a wider readership, this edition makes such an approach more possible than ever before, and I look forward to the encounters and conversations that will follow.

INTRODUCTION

Jean Toomer

Striking Experience in the South and Southwest

They will come southwestward, not on horseback or in a covered wagon but driving a motorcar. Even so they will strike experience here, as man ever does when his heart is freshly given to a place.

—JEAN TOOMER, **A Drama of the Southwest**, 1935

So speaks the Interpreter in Jean Toomer's *A Drama of the Southwest*, the incomplete or partially lost 1935 play, published here for the first time. The Interpreter's prophecy applies to the Elliot family, who will alight from their car in the next scene, and also to the whole phenomenon of the automobile tourists and part-year residents who are the latest of many waves of journeyers who have flocked to Taos, New Mexico, since the late nineteenth century. Under the banner of an optimistic promise that "they will strike experience here," the play pursues the question of what kind of experience, insight, or relationship to place these visitors may find, despite the motorcar journey that might seem to diminish the seriousness of their migrations or pilgrimages.

The Interpreter's proclamation is also a defense of creating from the stance of an outsider. It can serve to justify not only *A Drama of the Southwest* but much of Toomer's creative output. It was from this vantage, not of the native son but of the invested sojourner, that he produced *Cane*, the 1923 text that marked him as a rising star in modernist and African American literature and upon which his literary reputation is founded to this day. *Cane* depicts a northern African American's encounter with black rural southern culture, particularly in the play *Kabnis*, which makes up the third part of the book. The short stories set in the South are often mistaken for an insider's writing about his own community, but Toomer produced *Cane* after only a three-month stay in rural Georgia. *Cane* is at its most self-conscious and modern when it foregrounds its northern narrator's primitivist desire to recover and preserve African American folk culture.[1] These dynamics of primitivism and patronage are applicable in New Mexico, too, for Harlem Renaissance patronage resembled and existed in the same social networks as modernist patronage of Native American and *Nuevomexicano* arts and culture around Taos and Santa Fe.[2] In this cultural context, and in the context of Toomer's long-term fascination with the possibilities and limitations of the position of the invested sojourner, Toomer's later work from New Mexico emerges not as curious late-career vagary but as a logical extension of *Cane*'s critique of modernity, racialization, and primitivism.

The Interpreter promises that an artist prospecting for experience may strike it not because of the duration of his tenure in the Southwest, nor birthright, land ownership, or ethnographic credentials, but merely because his "heart is freshly given to a place." *A Drama of the Southwest* examines the desires of an entire taxonomy of outsiders who came to Taos around the cusp of the twentieth century: tourists in search of novelty, male and female artists, neonatives who stayed and became hosts and patrons to the other newcomers.[3] This self-conscious staging of the quest for experience in Taos describes the problematic nature of the roles then available for entering this land. I use the word "sojourner" for Toomer himself to suggest that he may have found the elusive other role that the play seeks. It is a word that acknowledges motion while taking its origin and its emphasis from the act of staying—temporarily. Scholars have paid much attention over the years to the idea of Toomer passing, running, fleeing, exiled; I propose shifting attention instead to how he dwelt, to his gift for opening himself to a new place with profound imagination and sympathy.[4]

Toomer never did buy land in New Mexico, but by the summer of 1935, when he was working on *A Drama of the Southwest*, he was on his fourth of six visits to the state. By then he was more intimate with it than a tourist, but he still lacked the deeper perspective of some of his local associates, notably neonatives like Georgia O'Keeffe and Mabel Dodge Luhan, the latter of whom he had stayed with during his first visit to New Mexico in the winter of 1925–1926.

Luhan had initially met Toomer in New York in 1925, where he was lecturing on the spiritual practices of the Russian mystic George I. Gurdjieff. Gurdjieff and Toomer taught that human beings could develop themselves by awakening their consciousnesses through self-study and communal living. Luhan was sufficiently attracted to Gurdjieffian philosophy—and to Toomer—that she determined to gather him into her New Mexico salon. During his visit to her, passion flared, at least on her side, and she entrusted him with $15,000 in support of the Gurdjieff work. The two talked of starting a Gurdjieff institute in Taos, but Gurdjieff himself demanded money to support instead the institute already established at Fontainebleau, France, and the fund was bled away over the years. This was such a grave disappointment to Luhan that it soured her relationship with Toomer and also, eventually, Toomer's relationship with Gurdjieff.

Nonetheless, Toomer visited New Mexico again in November of 1931, shortly after his marriage to Margery Latimer and fresh from that summer's experiment in communal living at Portage, Wisconsin. By this time, he had completed a draft of his long poem, "Blue Meridian," which uses vital imagery of the southwestern landscape and Pueblo dance to name "the great red race" as one of many strains to be mixed into the "new people . . . called Americans."[5]

> In a land of flaming earth and torrent-rains,
> Of red sea-plains and majestic mesas,
> At sunset from a purple hill
> The Gods came down;
> They serpentined into pueblo,
> And a white-robed priest
> Danced with them five days and nights.[6]

This vivid verb, serpentined, evokes a line of dancers, blurring the line between gods and dancers representing gods. Several times in "Blue Meridian," Pueblo dance is powerfully associated with images of fertility: it is "an example of the organic," of mysteries enacted in an age of facts; the priests performing a Corn Dance are "daubed with mud to grace the fecund," in stark contrast to the poem's depiction of the urban activity of white culture as futile and sterile. In this Pueblo connection to a "sacred earth" lies the generative power that would allow "a new America . . . To be taken as a golden grain / And lifted as the wheat of our bodies."[7]

During this period, both as expressed in "Blue Meridian" and in writings related to his marriage to Latimer, Toomer's vision for new Americans was rooted explicitly in racial mixing.[8] Margery Latimer Toomer shared her husband's vision for making a new American race by their union. She wrote exultantly to a friend about the marriage and her pregnancy in similarly bountiful, gold-colored imagery: "My stomach seems leaping with golden children, millions of them, and my head is purged of darkness and struggle and misery."[9] During their time in New Mexico, the Toomers stayed in Santa Fe with friends of Luhan and explored the possibility of settling and continuing the Gurdjieff work there, but they found depression-era economic conditions unsuited to forming an institute or community.[10] They then moved to Carmel, California, to another artist's community, but were harried by negative publicity over their interracial marriage. Finally, they returned to Chicago, where Margery died on August 16, 1932, after giving birth to their daughter, Margery ("Argie") Toomer Latimer.

In the summer of 1934, Toomer came to New Mexico again, this time to catch up with Marjorie Content, whom he had met in New York in the spring of 1934 and would wed in Taos in September. Content was more familiar with the Southwest than he, having traveled in the region extensively since 1931 and having lived on the Apache, Navajo, and Papago (Tohono O'odham) Reservations from 1933–1934, working as a photographer for the Bureau of Indian Affairs. Content had traveled ahead of Toomer, driving to New Mexico with Georgia O'Keeffe in June (her correspondence with Toomer during that journey forms appendix D of this volume).

Toomer arrived a month later, ready to embark on a new phase of life. He had just finished the task of arranging Margery Latimer's correspondence for possible publication, so in a sense he had closed the book on his first marriage and the intense devotion to the Gurdjieff work from which it had grown. Though Toomer's definitive break with Gurdjieff would not come until early in 1935, their quarrels over Luhan's money in 1933–1934 had already set the scene.[11] When he crossed the Mississippi, that threshold of the West, Toomer reported to Content:

> I recited—almost chanted—that part of "The Blue Meridian" which has to do with the great brown river. My emotions just suddenly remembered it. I felt I was engaged in a sacred ritual, in a prayer, in a song of triumph!

The Mississippi, sister of the Ganges,
Main artery of earth in the western world,
Is waiting to become
In the spirit of America
A sacred river,
Whoever lifts that river
Lifts himself and all America,
Whoever lifts himself
Makes that great brown river smile;
The blood of earth and the blood of man
Course swifter and rejoice when we spiritualize.[12]

Here Toomer recruits the older work to mark a new crossing in his life. He is leaving behind the midwestern social circle he had shared with Latimer, his in-laws, with whom he lived while preparing her letters for publication, and his daughter, whom he visited only briefly while in Chicago. Even within this letter's texture, the Mississippi is a threshold, the place where Toomer leaves behind the minutiae of travel logistics and allows his language to soar as he moves toward his reunion with Content. In marking his westward passage with poetry at such a crucial geographic point, Toomer also marks his return to the southwestern earth and perhaps even to his hopes for New Mexico as a meeting and mingling place of races. Emily Lutenski has argued that, around this time, Toomer saw the Southwest as a place with unique possibilities for standing outside the black/white racial binary prevalent in so much of the nation, operating as it did on different axes of Native American, Hispanic, and Anglo, and with a different relationship to hybridity—the mestizo.[13]

The following summer, when he composed *A Drama of the Southwest* in a small, rented adobe house outside of Taos, Toomer was no longer the newlywed of 1931 who dreamed of heading up a Gurdjieffian community and who hoped his own marriage would help bring about a new race in America. Nor had he yet so fully repudiated that vision as he would in his New Mexico notebook of 1947, when he discarded the dream of a new American race (calling it "the mingling of bodies in copulation") as untenable because it could not be undertaken rapidly enough to prevent a third world war and pinned his hopes instead on spiritual transformation, concluding that "men and women with Christ-like qualities" would need to "appear in every country," lest "the atom bombs . . . begin to fall."[14]

Writing *A Drama of the Southwest* between these two moments, Toomer highlights both the promises and the limitations of the artists' community in Taos. As the character Tom Elliot's descriptions of his feelings upon crossing Raton Pass in scenes 4 and 7 show, it still seems possible that the physical setting in New Mexico can inspire feelings of transcendence. Yet of all the artists in the play, only the poet Lillian Range succeeds in actually accomplishing any work during her time in Taos. Still Tom and his wife, Grace, seek to settle there, imagining it as a landscape in which he could be productive and valuing, as they did, the looser social conventions they felt were part of it. As Tom writes of their rented house to a friend, "Feature Tom and Grace living on the highway in a native house a stone's throw from an auto camp! In no other place would we do it. And, I might add, in no other place could it be done as it is done here. This country is so great that it reconciles everything."[15] Tom seems to be reveling in the incongruity and impropriety of living in such proximity to the unknown populations of tourists or even migrants who might pass through a Depression-era auto camp. At other moments, Tom and Grace are not nearly so ostentatiously open-minded, as when they consider whether the "Mexican children" their daughter plays with present a risk of physical or moral contagion. Such incidents and the brief appearances of domestic and day laborers in *A Drama of the Southwest* point to the dynamic that Lois Rudnick has commented on, in which an influx of new residents, tourists, and neo-natives exacerbated existing interethnic tensions in the region. Indian enthusiasts who came to Taos to be near the Pueblo sometimes also supported Hispanic artists, craftspeople, and laborers, but frequently also worked against impoverished Hispanic communities when championing Native American claims to land and resources.[16] In *A Drama of the Southwest*, as in life, those who came to Taos with utopian dreams lived there imperfectly.

Toomer registered his ambivalence toward the landscape in ways that will feel familiar to readers of *Cane*. In both *Cane* and *A Drama of the Southwest*, works Toomer produced after periods of deeply invested sojourning, giving one's heart to a place does not mean adoring it unreservedly. In a 1934 letter to Content, he writes of New Mexico:

> That country is surely my country too. I have a love for it. Yet, as you know, I hate it also. . . . It is almost as if, ages ago, I suffered deeply in it—and a memory of that suffering sometimes stirs in the regions of myself far below consciousness. I want to found and build a world there. Also I feel that no good can come of it to me or anyone I love.[17]

Like his character Kabnis, who despises being moved by the beauty of the Georgia night because such feelings draw him to greater intimacy with an often hostile and dangerous land, Toomer is gripped with a powerful combination of newness and intimacy, of love and hate for New Mexico. His southwestern sojourns of 1934 and 1935, then, were not a retreat or a flight for Toomer. They were a return to the unsettling position that he recognized as his position of greatest creative power, that of one whose heart is "freshly given to a place."

A Drama of the Southwest in Jean Toomer's Career

A Drama of the Southwest opens with a night scene at Taos Pueblo, proceeds through a philosophical dialogue on a rooftop to a brief speech by a chorus-like figure, the Interpreter, and ends with an extended scene of the arrival of Grace and Tom Elliot in Taos. Various concerns are introduced: the Elliots' adjustment to Taos, their longing for a place of their own, Tom's discomfort with the women of Taos, and the marital troubles of their friend John Woodward. The play's second day is bookended by the Elliot family's dubious interactions with Pueblo culture. In the morning, Tom Elliot performs an imitation of a Pueblo dance outside the house, and the landladies warn his wife, Grace, that he is intruding upon sacred traditions. That evening, the Elliots bring two friends to Taos Pueblo to hear the Indians sing, but they are disappointed by silence. Tom's dancing is the talk of Taos Plaza on the third morning in scene 11.[18] The Woodward marital troubles are taken up again in scenes 12 and 13 when Helen Woodward confides in Grace that her husband believes she is unfaithful and Tom attempts to meddle in the relationship by confronting Helen's mother and chasing John Woodward in his car, writing marital melodrama across the landscape. The play does not end but rather cuts off in the final scene with the Elliots receiving news of land they hope to buy and preparing to welcome a Communist for tea.

Despite its incompleteness, the play merits attention because it can help reorient our view of Jean Toomer's canonical and late works, and because it offers scholars of the American Southwest another picture of the Mabel Dodge Luhan years in Taos. Toomer writes sensitively of one of the great limitations of that artistic community—the barriers that cultures of connoisseurship and patronage throw up against genuine intercultural contact, suggesting that his experience on the receiving end of primitivism-tinged Harlem Renaissance–era interracial patronage primed him to criticize that dynamic in New Mexico. His writings also attend with raw honesty and humor to the trials of the male ego in an artists' community rich in female luminaries.

Though *A Drama of the Southwest* should not be mistaken for pure autobiography, it is a hitherto undervalued text in its cultural, literary, and historical contexts. The play dispels several myths about Toomer's late career and his literary output from New Mexico. Despite widespread reports of the failure of a playwright and of an author who "abandoned his lyrical vein" when he ceased to write of rural Georgia, *A Drama of the Southwest* delivers astute social commentary, contests of ideas, and moments of great beauty.[19] The play also provides, like D. H. Lawrence's *Altitude* or Mabel Dodge Luhan's memoirs, an image of the social world of the artists who mined Taos for creative and spiritual renewal in the early twentieth century. The failure thus far to value *A Drama of the Southwest* for its portrayal of this important moment in New Mexico's artistic history flows from both an undervaluing of the outsider's position and a knee-jerk skepticism about Toomer's authority to write from New Mexico, and these positions are ones that the play itself can help unsettle.

We do not, strictly speaking, value Toomer for his testimony. We value him for receiving and assembling a richly varied collection of experiences and cultural, historical, and literary influences into beautiful fictions. Jean Toomer in New Mexico in the 1930s retains that receptiveness, the outsider's keen eye, and the ability to make us feel he writes of a place with authority. To watch Toomer at work in New Mexico is to become more sensitive to the skills he brought to Georgia.

By demanding that Toomer be of the region about which he writes, we invest in precisely the kind of self-important expertise and authority to speak for a place that *A Drama of the Southwest* holds up for skepticism. This is the false authority that allows Tom Elliot to make pronouncements about Pueblo spiritual practices as long as no actual Pueblo Indians are present and that causes John Woodward to dismiss strong southwestern women as shrill wildcats and to speculate on menopausal symptoms in the lesbian landladies. It is not enough for our criticism to vet an author's credentials to speak with singular authority about a place and its lifeways. A more delicate negotiation is required, in which we remain open to the possibility that outsiders like Tom and John (and, by extension, Toomer himself) can strike deep experience in a new place, while at the same time recognizing that their assertions about the meaning of a place are always subject to undermining and interrogation—interrogation at which the dramatic form excels and that Toomer uses to good effect both in *Kabnis* and in *A Drama of the Southwest*.

If it gives us pause to see Toomer deeply engaged and firmly emplaced in the Southwest instead of in a rural landscape in the South, it is a pause in which we can recognize how long-exaggerated Toomer's southern regionalism has been, and how that exaggerated regionalism is entwined with the latest round of attempts to shore up Toomer's pre-1923 claim to blackness, the better to accuse him of later abandoning it in passing.[20] Claims of southernness, functioning as coded claims of race identity, are involved in arguments that inscribe *Cane* as a classic of African American literature by differentiating it from and disparaging the rest of Toomer's life and work. This tendency to condemn Toomer's late work cannot possibly heap greater laurels upon *Cane* than the book earns for itself, but it has wreaked editorial havoc on the late work. Toomer's achievements in the Southwest in the 1930s do not threaten or dilute his achievements in the Georgia stories or the urban stories of 1923 once our understanding of the merit of those stories is uncoupled from a scholarly quest for racial authenticity. Toomer need not write from the South, or from a moment of wholehearted black identity, to write with insight and clarity of vision. *A Drama of the Southwest* teaches us as much, for Toomer has no great claim on the Southwest, any more than the other modernists who embraced and claimed New Mexico as a spiritual home. Nor does he need such a claim. We risk blinding ourselves to Toomer's artistry when we cast his creativity as reportage and his sojourning as belonging.

Tom Elliot in Taos

The setting of the first scene is Taos Pueblo, the iconic centuries-old adobe village northeast of Taos. Toomer's prose description of this place is so rich in its geographic specificity that it is hard to imagine the cardboard Taos or projector-screen night sky that could stage it. "The only sounds," initially, are those of a creek that flows from Blue Lake toward the Rio Grande. A creek might be staged in some fashion, but the geographical knowledge concerning its origin and destination is harder to convey.[21]

The extravagance of these stage directions does not necessarily mean that *A Drama of the Southwest* is a closet drama, a play meant for reading but never for performance. Toomer actively sought staging opportunities for *Kabnis*, and comparing the two plays suggests that, throughout his career, Toomer was willing to lavish gorgeous metaphorical language (the moon as a "white child that sleeps upon the treetops of the forest. . . . Black mother sways, holding a white child on her bosom") and supravisual geographical information ("Somewhere, far off in the straight line of his sight, is Augusta. . . . And hours, hours north, why not say a lifetime north? Washington sleeps") upon his stage directions.[22] In the text of *Kabnis*, seemingly unstageable stage directions offer up not a setting but a vision of Kabnis seeing the place. His fears of lynching, his consciousness of a history and ongoing reality of interracial sexual coercion, and his longing for cities to the north all shape what he sees in the Georgia night.

The opening scene of *A Drama of the Southwest*, too, has stage directions that alter perceptions of a landscape. The staging challenge that these rich and geographically intensive directions present could be resolved by the simple use of narration, a choice that would be much in keeping with *A Drama of the Southwest*'s third scene, which consists entirely of a speech by the chorus-like Interpreter. With the help of such narration, the unnamed watercourse at the center of the scene becomes "the creek that comes down from Blue Lake," and so situates Taos Pueblo's absolute dependence on its water in an arid mountain ecosystem.[23] To a listener with some local knowledge, the naming of the creek's source at Blue Lake connects the scene to a religious and political present. Blue Lake is legible in religious terms as the sacred origin site of the Pueblo people, and in political terms as the locus of a then-ongoing struggle by the Pueblo to regain the site, which had been guaranteed to them in 1848 under the Treaty of Guadalupe Hidalgo but was appropriated as part of Carson National Forest by Theodore Roosevelt in 1906. At that time, Pueblo advocates were given a promise—not long kept—that exclusive Pueblo Indian use would be preserved. There are environmental implications in the image of the creek, too, touching on the precarious nature of desert life. Today, tribal control of Blue Lake and its outflow stream assures that the water in Taos Creek (the Rio Pueblo de Taos) is safe to drink; in 1935, that water supply was vulnerable to pollution from upstream mining and logging on federally managed land.

The status of this land is raised again in the second scene at Taos Pueblo when Lillian asks of the canyon that leads up to Blue Lake, "Is it Indian land?" and Tom answers somewhat ambiguously, "Legally, and by right of living."[24] Whether or not Tom is fully aware of it, the legal right and the right of living created by six thousand years of continuous use do not make for entire sovereignty in Taos. Valid though the Pueblo's legal claim to the land is, it will take until 1965 for the federal Indian Claims Commission to rule that the appropriation of the land was unjust.[25] While pressing for this outcome, Taos Pueblo contended with US Forest Service policies that included resource extraction, unaffordable fees for grazing permits that disrupted centuries of previous use, and the cutting of trails to encourage recreational use of the sacred site by outsiders. Even the "good trout fishing" that Tom reports as available in the stream is indicative of the Forest Service's disregard for the religious privacy of the sacred site and the promise of exclusive use. Blue Lake and its stream held no trout until the waters were stocked in 1916 by the supervisor of the national forest in an effort to make the area more inviting to recreation.[26]

The play's first movement is a gathering at this crucial and contested water source, when, after a long silence, a group of Pueblo men emerge from the buildings on either side of the water, greet each other in their own language, and gather on a bridge to sing three Taos songs. Thus, after holding his audience in prolonged anticipation for the first line of his play, Toomer provides a line of greeting that most listeners will not understand, and then directs their attention to the Pueblo songs. Just what is meant by such an opening? On the surface, there is an element of local color, an auditory sampling of the type of song and dance that tourists had long come to the Southwest to see. Yet by placing the Native American art form on the same stage as the domestic drama that follows it, Toomer makes a claim for the equivalent valuation of those two art forms. This is in keeping with the interest Toomer shows in Native Americans throughout his New Mexico notebooks, and with his project—visible even in his first drama, *Natalie Mann*—of elevating music and dance as fundamental ways for drama to advance characterization, plot development, and symbolic meaning.[27] Certainly Toomer expects a great deal from the three Taos songs, for, after them, his stage directions instruct: "Then silence again . . . and life becomes existence again . . . and existence, focused for a time in a group of singing men, expands to the mountain and the close stars."[28]

This opening scene allows the audience to see a representation of Taos Pueblo and hear the Taos songs without extensive framing or expectations. For the remainder of the play, they will watch as the Anglo main characters arrive in Taos and quest after this very experience: the chance to sit in darkness and hear the Taos songs. The effect is not quite to deflate the fetishized Taos songs. The stage direction describing how existence was "focused for a time in a group of singing men" is an instruction for profound attention, perhaps even breathless fascination and enjoyment.[29] Without making the decision to take an Indian Detour—one of those famous prepackaged motorcar tours that shepherded railroad passengers through historic and cultural sites in northern New Mexico in the 1920s and '30s—to participate in a tourism transaction built upon primitivism and patronage, without lusting after and seeking out the novelty or profound mystery that Native song might offer, the audience has simply encountered the performance. Toomer has made the audience of *A Drama of the Southwest* into accidental tourists.

As the play unfolds, it stages that local network of power and patronage through a continuum of acts of tourism, viewership, invasion, and cultural appropriation, but the audience is implicated in these acts from the very first scene. The next scene, a rooftop dialogue at dawn between Ubeam Riseling (the Taos Visionary) and Buckter T. Fact (the Taos Kid), develops this theme. Ubeam is "a figure wrapped in a blanket like an Indian, though he is not an Indian—a poet, import, and visionary, a person of some depth and dignity who does not belong to the art colony because he is above art."[30] Names in *A Drama of the Southwest* are often suggestive, if not outright allegorical. Ubeam Riseling's name conjures any number of associations: sunbeams; Riesling grapes or wine; the steel universal beams (I-beams, or U-beams, as they are sometimes called) that undergird so much non-adobe frame construction.

The name marks him as the intellectual W. E. B. Du Bois to Buckter T. Fact's Booker T. Washington, but Riseling's name is ghosted by a fear that Riseling's poetic regional vision may be impotent or infertile. ("Risling" is also a word for a male horse with one or more testicles retained within the body cavity.) Ubeam and Buck Fact, the dungaree-clad butcher and proletarian described as "below art," represent two ways of looking at Taos, two possibilities for its promotion and, indeed, its uplift.

When Ubeam rapturously declares of Taos, "This is the roof of the world," Buck Fact immediately converts the observation into a hard fact: "Elevation six thousand nine hundred odd feet."[31] He then spins into a marketing rap: "Over Raton Pass . . . down Cimarron Canyon . . . and you, too, my dear tourists, will be here on the roof of the world, even as he and I."[32] Buck Fact's welcome to the tourists could be delivered with showmanship or sarcasm. He calls them "queer birds" and jokes about Mabel Dodge Luhan, "a writer who sees to it that her history is better known" than that of the nearby pueblo.[33] When Ubeam describes the Taos Indians as "magnetiz[ing] Taos" until "the entire world comes," Buck Fact sees a frivolous movement ("Why should anyone come all this way to get dust in his eyes?") that is nonetheless an important economic force: "As for me, it means a job." Luhan's self-promotion and her promotion of Taos make Pueblo culture function as a magnet for tourists. This is not what Ubeam had in mind when he described the Indians as charming the mountains, filling the canyons with echoes, and magnetizing Taos. He responds by trying to take back his metaphor, to connect the idea of magnetism to a noneconomic form of productivity:

> Taos magnetizes, hence it must create. In the days of the great seasons, after this awful winter of man, something very great will come to growth in the Southwest, uniting the geography and the people, the earth and mankind, this planet and the universe.[34]

The notion of Taos Pueblo or Mabel Dodge Luhan as magnetic is frequently repeated in contemporary and present-day writing about the region's artists' colony of that era. One senses Toomer's considerable investment in the Taos of Ubeam Riseling's dream vision, a Taos with much to teach the world. The last word in the scene is the vague vatic prediction that "something very great will come to growth in the Southwest," upheld by the gnomic pronouncement, "Remember that the cactus blooms."[35] Yet even after he gives this last word to Ubeam Riseling, Toomer undermines him with a gesture. The next rooftop dialogue begins when Ubeam "rises to a stand, facing east, and lifts his right arm in a gesture suggestive of the Nazi salute" and cries, "Hail to thee, rising sun!"[36] Is this the visionary in whom we trusted? Even in 1935, with the connotations of Nazism perhaps running more toward hostility to Communism and ominous militarization than genocide and war, Ubeam's gesture casts a pall over the enthusiastic vision he presents for Taos's development. Even in the most innocuous of readings, Ubeam has made himself ridiculous. "Sit down," Buck Fact tells him dryly, "the sun rose three hours ago."[37] This small exchange is part of a pattern of undermining and deflating that Toomer's play deploys against those characters—Tom chief among them—whom it might be most tempting to identify as pronouncing the play's or the playwright's view.[38]

Any proclamation in *A Drama of the Southwest* is mediated by speaker and audience, just as any revelation to be found in Taos must be negotiated within a network of tourism and patronage, in which the earnest questing of pilgrims is always at risk of being cheapened or turned to dust. In the third scene, the Interpreter again strikes a tone of breathless prophecy while setting the stage for the arrival of the main characters:

> People are coming, people from the East. They will find this land pre-inhabited, even as the first desert was; but they will come as if discovering Taos, planting their flag in this high earth. They will come southwestward, not on horseback or in a covered wagon but driving a motorcar. Even so they will strike experience here, as man ever does when his heart is freshly given to a place.[39]

This last sentence functions, I have argued, as a manifesto justifying creation by outsiders, people from the East like Toomer himself and like Tom Elliot. But the Interpreter establishes a crucial distance from such figures by noting their tendency to misinterpret New Mexico's empty-seeming land. He or she credits these people from the East as coming "as if discovering Taos," not as discoverers; he associates their arrival with "planting their flag," placing them within a history of imperialist projections into the region by Spain and the United States. He warns the audience not to forget that the land is "preinhabited," no matter how passionately the Elliots will speak the language of discovery.

The Interpreter's admonition asks that we look backward as well as forward. The first scene of *A Drama of the Southwest* is its only one comprising exclusively Native American characters. Furthermore, there are no technologies in the scene that serve as temporal markers. If an audience facing the set as Toomer describes it were watching the scene unfold at Taos Pueblo itself, they would be standing on the plaza with the San Geronimo chapel and the ruins of the earlier church both invisible behind them. Thus, the absence of these structures from the set gives no clue to the date; the scene might easily have been set in 1618, before the building of the first church at the pueblo, as in 1935. Unmoored in the centuries as it is, the play's first scene emphasizes the long duration of human habitation in Taos even as it tempts viewers toward the fallacy of aboriginal timelessness. It then initiates a jarring contrast between the still evening of song and the morning dialogue on automobile tourism. The audience is invited to misapprehend the chronological setting and then to revise those misapprehensions in a process that may ultimately leave them questioning the trustworthiness of their own sensations of discovery and the voyeuristic ethics of finding themselves camped upon Taos Pueblo's plaza hearing those songs.

Moments like the Interpreter's speech argue for a self-consciousness in *A Drama of the Southwest*'s staging of the eastern intellectuals' quest for experience in New Mexico. By the time the Elliot family arrives in Taos, the audience is well prepared to regard them as the latest in a long series of newcomers and to contextualize their activities as part of a commonplace touristic trend, perhaps even a suspect one. The fourth scene, and the real plot arc of the play, opens with two landladies preparing an adobe house for the Elliot family as roofers work above them. Given local labor patterns, the men on the roof are surely Pueblo Indian or Nuevomexicano, like the nameless and silent "Mexican woman" applying *tierra blanca* to the walls of the cottage and the real maids, gardeners, and other nearly invisible menial workers employed by neonatives in Taos. Here, however, the workmen on the roof refuse to consent to their invisibility. It would be possible to stage them so they can be seen by the audience, or merely to provide evidence of their presence—their preinhabitation of Taos—in the form of the much-romanticized adobe plaster that rains onto the heads of the interlocutors as the roofers pound and stomp above.

The landladies are soon interrupted by another character who, like the Interpreter, forewarns the audience against attending to Tom Elliot with too much credulity. Both a typescript and a holograph version of this scene survive, and in each one, before Tom and Grace Elliot arrive, Hanna Gow delivers a swift and brutal character assessment of him to the landladies: "He thinks he's God's own man. One of those real men who tame shrews and all that."[40] Tom and Hanna immediately flourish their disagreements about the women in Taos when she teases him about the status of his revolution "against female Fascism."

Hanna cuts to the heart of Tom's insecurities by alluding to the discomfort that egotistical male artists feel in an art community particularly known for female leadership. Flannery Burke's 2008 study, *From Greenwich Village to Taos*, describes how Luhan and Mary Austin leveraged their patronage and perceptions of a special connection to primitive New Mexico for local and national cultural capital. In Burke's reading, D. H. Lawrence and Carl Van Vechten were (like Toomer's Tom Elliot) latecomers to the New Mexico art scene who might have engaged there more fully had they not chafed to find the position of cultural authority already occupied by women.[41] The female artists and art patrons of Taos, then, form another layer of preinhabitation that is inconvenient or threatening to men like Tom Elliot who would like to set themselves up as discoverers.

Further hints that Tom's authority on New Mexico is more aspirational than actual frequently emerge with reference to his daughter, Betty. Betty never appears on stage, and she only appears in her parents' minds when New Mexico offers her some new peril. Otherwise, they allow her to wander where she will outside the house. "I've hardly been out, except to snatch Betty off the road," Tom confides in a letter, meaning to describe how hard he has been working, but inadvertently revealing something about his parenting.[42] He and his wife express concerns about black widow spiders, about Betty crossing the cattle guard to play with the Mexican children who live nearby, and about the cars on the road into which she wanders so freely. All of these worries foreshadow one of these various dangers coming to fruition. If such a climactic scene existed (or survived), we would learn much about how the play judges the elder Elliots' ability to read the social and ecological landscape of Taos. Tom's arrogance, and the mounting critique of male modernists who would set themselves up as authorities on Taos, however, does not bode well for Betty.

In Toomer's play, Tom Elliot's tone-deaf efforts to assert expertise in matters of local fauna, Pueblo dance, and sacred geography are contrasted with his wife's more subtle efforts to interpolate between the Pueblo community, the neonative landladies, and her family. The landladies expect Grace Elliot to begin this diplomatic work on the second morning when they find Tom outside the house, greeting the dawn by performing his own rendition of a Pueblo dance. What are we to make of this moment? Where and when did this Taos newcomer learn such a thing? In this 1930s context, Tom has just revealed himself as a Native American hobbyist—one of many largely white Americans who, through scouting, camps, fairs, and other venues, incorporated playing at Indianness into their concept of recreation or right living, or even used it to forge an antimodern American identity. Toomer would have come into contact with such circles through Marjorie Content: her friend Ralph Hubbard was a renowned leader and teacher of Native American dance lore.[43] It is perhaps not entirely unusual for this era, then, for a newly arrived visitor to Taos to act in what he viewed as appropriately local fashion.

As interpreted by Toomer's play though, not everyone in 1930s Taos finds such behavior acceptable. One landlady exclaims, "He was wonderful," while the other warns her and Grace, "You mustn't encourage such antics in men. The Indians' dances are sacred to them. Mr. Elliot will be ashamed of himself."[44] Tom shows no signs of such shame yet, but his dancing is soon the talk of Taos Plaza and may well be the reason for his future rebuff at Taos Pueblo.

Grace, more experienced at living in Taos than her husband and friends, is chameleon-like in her ability to communicate with other visitors and with the neonative population, which derives cachet from intimacy with and understanding of Native Americans. Speaking with the landladies, Grace is quick to assert that the Taos Indians are no exotic spectacle, but are people among whom she has friends and with whom she can sympathize. "Imagine having strange people descend on you at all hours of the day, and poke about," she says.[45] She might have included all hours of the night, too, considering that she and Tom have been promising to take their friends Lillian Range and Bill Bryne to hear the Taos Indians sing and that she plans, that very evening, to lay siege to a private dwelling until they hear the songs.

The extent to which one can live in Taos without exotifying one's neighbors is crucial to identity in *A Drama of the Southwest*. The scene that follows Tom's ill-advised dancing is a crowd scene in Taos Plaza in which Toomer's stage directions describe seven distinct groups of people, a taxonomy of inhabitants and visitors that begins with Native Americans and ends with tourists.[46] The tourists, "they of recent arrival and soon departure," are "dressed in all manner of garb" but "are distinguishable from all the others by the sort of nervous curiosity which lays hold of our countrymen when they are sighting and seeing what they believe to be exotic."[47] Believing others to be exotic is as important as transience in identifying the tourist, and Toomer's coinage of "sighting and seeing" in place of "sightseeing" splits that action in two: a restless "sighting" that carries the thrill of discovery and the violence of gun sights, and "seeing," which seems to offer little insight, only a glimpse into the tourists' own preconceptions. By breaking apart sightseeing in this manner, Toomer makes clear how a tourist's gaze functions to make "sights"—objectified spectacles—out of people and places. The tourists, Buck Fact's "queer birds," are certainly held up for ridicule here as the people who behave worse than any other group in Taos, but it is difficult to trust Tom Elliot's sense of his own difference from them. His days, moving from Taos Plaza to Taos Pueblo, cover the same itinerary as the Taos day on a classic Indian Detour trip.

The Elliots' quest to hear the Taos songs reaches its disappointing denouement on the play's second night when it brings the action back to where it began, at Taos Pueblo. Tom, Grace, Lillian, and Bill settle near the stream on their blankets to hear the songs that Tom and Grace have been promising to their guests. The four wait, but no one comes to sing. Even as each passing moment of silence casts further doubt on the Elliots' self-appointed status as local Indian experts, Grace and Bill strive to put their knowledge and connoisseurship of Pueblo culture on display.

> LILLIAN: I haven't seen a dance. Do they dance well here?
> GRACE: Not as well as at some of the other pueblos.
> BRYNE: Everyone says the Domingo corn dance is the one to see.
> GRACE: It is intense and beautiful, one of the most impressive, but the tourists spoil it.[48]

Grace wins this exchange when she gives Bill a subtle slap with her scorn for the tourists at the Santo Domingo dance.[49] To call it the best is to have a tourist's taste.

When showing off for a tourist or short-term visitor like Lillian, Grace and Tom try to appear like more sophisticated and knowledgeable versions of tourists: they know the places, the songs, and the dances that no one else does. Striving to fill the empty time, Tom imparts information in a headlong rush, lecturing his wife and friends on Pueblo spiritual practices, their relationship with landscape, and the sacredness of Blue Lake. (In an earlier scene, he remarks to Lillian that at Blue Lake, "the Indians have dances which no white man has ever seen," and she responds, perhaps ominously, "I'd love to go."[50])

Due to the incompleteness of *A Drama of the Southwest*, it is not clear whether these persistent mentions of Blue Lake are setting up a later plot event like an actual expedition to intrude upon the sacred site, or if they are only Toomer's efforts to keep New Mexico geography in the foreground. Even if nothing else comes of it, the discussion of Blue Lake serves to develop Tom's character and his relationship to the Pueblo Indians. When Lillian asks him, "What is Blue Lake that it fascinates you so?" Tom, who can rarely keep any utterance under a paragraph, is at an uncharacteristic loss for words. "I couldn't tell you," he says.[51] Here Tom admits to being unable to answer two questions: What is Blue Lake? He has not been and cannot really know. Why does it fascinate him? Even his own fascination with the Pueblo Indians is not articulable or sufficiently examined.

Everyone sits in silence for a moment after Tom's admission of ignorance on the subject of Blue Lake, until Lillian observes, "No singing yet." The Elliots look sillier and sillier, unable to deliver the promised after-dinner spectacle to their guests. Grace's flustered reply is, "There must be some reason, but I don't know it. This is most unusual. Perhaps we should wait no longer."[52] She is the first to catch the drift that they might not be welcome, and charged as she was with reining in Tom's mimicry of Pueblo dance, she has some idea of why. The silence at the pueblo is Toomer's censure of Tom's behavior. Toomer denies his characters the long-sought performance he has already granted to the audience in the first scene. But Tom's self-absorption bears him easily over the disappointment. Rhapsodizing about the mere nearness of the pueblo, Tom declares, "There is a leaven here which the more fortunate of us may share and use for our own baking."[53] Tom's impulse is extractive. Indeed, Toomer first wrote that the fortunate could "take away" the leaven, and he substituted "share" afterward.[54] Tom and the other visitors to Taos see in Pueblo culture a flickering mirror of their own ideals: now a political model for communal society; now a source of spiritual wisdom. Bill defines the Soviet project as "trying to manufacture . . . in a few years" what "took centuries to grow" in New Mexico, while Tom, interested in spiritual matters, inverts the usual primitivist developmental hierarchy when he suggests the Pueblo community as a model of a "mature civilization" from which his "boisterous, child-active civilization" might learn the art of contemplation and so grow a soul.[55]

All of these constructions of meaning are briefly punctured when an older Pueblo man approaches the group and engages them in seemingly uninformative small talk. "Will the boys sing tonight?" Tom asks him, striking a note of breezy familiarity or even insulting infantilization when referring to a group that consisted, by all other descriptions, of adult men. "Sing every night," and "Don't know. The boys sing every night," is the man's twice-repeated reply to Tom's further queries, providing him with only an echo of his assumptions.[56] The real Pueblo Indian moves off stage, once more leaving Tom to field the questions of his companions and spin his elaborate theories of the meaning of Pueblo culture. As Lillian puts it at the conclusion of the scene at the pueblo, "If they had sung, we would have heard them. In their silence, we heard ourselves."[57]

This observation is not the first time *A Drama of the Southwest* locates the value of intercultural contact as lying in productive estrangements and seeing the self differently rather than in seeing difference. Grace, too, values interaction with the Pueblo people for the mirror that community could turn upon Anglo society. While discussing the prominent placement of the town dump in Taos with the landladies, Grace observes, "Who can miss it? Right on the highway. Couldn't civic pride find a more concealed spot? Or is Taos proud of its consumption of canned goods?"—then, enlisting the Taos Indians to her side as she criticizes her community, she adds, "I once went to a dance where the Indians symbolized the presence of the white man by a heap of tin cans." Mary Austin related a similar anecdote in her 1924 article, "Cults of the Pueblos."[58] It is not clear whether Toomer witnessed similar performances himself, is leaning upon Austin's article, or is merely repeating an anecdote popular in their shared circle of New Mexico artists. In any event, their paired recourse to the depressing detail of the white man represented by a heap of tin cans indicates that both writers believe the Anglo culture can be fruitfully disciplined by the whip of Pueblo laughter. In this moment, the Pueblo performers are elevated above the status of objects of primitivist interest, or symbols to be invested with meaning, and given credit for their roles as cultural critics and interlocutors.

Even in quotation, Native American voices are rare in *A Drama of the Southwest*, perhaps meaningfully so. The recursive experience of trying to listen to Native Americans and hearing only one's self is also reminiscent of Toomer's definition of tourists, those people who move about in a state of "nervous curiosity . . . sighting and seeing what they believe to be exotic." It is thus possible to read Lillian Range's statement along the same lines as Hanna Gow's objections to Tom—as a withering character assessment of the man who "thinks he's God's own man" and who sat before the pueblo and did the most talking when he might have been listening. If this is the case, Tom has failed in his efforts to become something more than a tourist, to escape the cycle of frantic motion in automobiles and superficial interactions with people whom he insists on exoticizing. It is also just possible, however, that Lillian does not mean to criticize herself and her friends when she observes that the group heard only itself. Certainly Tom experiences the evening as a gift. The scene ends with a benediction, as Tom calls back, "Indians of pueblo, you will not hear me, but thank you—and goodnight."[59]

Tom, despite every rebuff, seems to have received some dose of the inspiration he sought at the pueblo, but his final words enact a moment of cross-cultural communication that misses its mark—the Taos Indians won't hear because Tom has chosen to speak to them when they are not even within earshot. This example of Tom's failure to dwell gracefully in Taos reinforces the play's skepticism of persons who would set themselves up as authorities on those whom they consider to be exotic or primitive.

Ultimately, *A Drama of the Southwest* suggests it is possible for Tom to find something of value in New Mexico—not an experience of approaching "authentic" Native American culture but an experience of his own discomfort and productive estrangement from the various local communities already inhabiting the region. While *A Drama of the Southwest* criticizes—and at times even ridicules—the desires and actions of tourists and other newcomers, it never rejects the premise that there are experiences worth seeking, if one can only learn how to open one's self to a place.

A Partial Key to the Characters

The semiautobiographical nature of *A Drama of the Southwest* may serve as an enticement to readers interested in the lives of Jean Toomer and his contemporaries in Taos. Readers have always been swift to identify Tom, Grace, and their daughter Betty as thinly veiled portraits of Jean Toomer, Marjorie Content, and Toomer's daughter Margery (Argie) Toomer Latimer, who turned three in the summer of 1935. Other characters present greater interpretive challenges.

HANNA GOW

Rudolph Byrd notes that Jean Toomer and Mabel Dodge Luhan were former lovers, and he identifies Hanna Gow as a spitefully unflattering portrait of Luhan, citing "all her Native American jewelry, shrillness and force."[60] But Byrd's reading takes the male characters' hostility toward Gow at face value and quotes John Woodward's description of her as a "wildcat" without examination.[61] In reality, Tom's approval of John's assessment ("Rub her right and she purrs. Rub her wrong and she claws") can serve to support Hanna's notion of Tom as a man who, much to the amusement of the women involved, thinks he can handle women. It is not safe to trust the male characters' descriptions of Hanna as the play's final word on her. She cuts a jaunty figure, making her entrance in a cowboy hat and boots; her horse is tied up off stage. Her banter, which includes such quips as, "I don't wish them any bad luck, but I hope they get drowned in floods," is a breath of fresh air in a work sometimes plagued by sagging dialogue.[62] There is thus ample evidence of this play liking Hanna a good deal more than Byrd gives it credit for. Hanna's aggressive stance toward Tom may make her Tom's antagonist, but it does not mark her as the play's antagonist or make Luhan and the Taos women the butt of the play's jokes.

Furthermore, the archive does not support a swift identification of Hanna Gow as Mabel Dodge Luhan. In the holograph, this character is called "Tough Girl." One year before her creation, in June 1934, while Marjorie Content and Georgia O'Keeffe drove to New Mexico, Content and Toomer kept up an energetic correspondence in which Toomer referred to the two traveling women by the nickname, "The Tough Girls."[63] Hanna's name in the holograph thus indicates that Toomer did not model Hanna upon Luhan, the friend, patron, or lover with whom he had a falling out over money, but instead modeled her after his new bride and O'Keeffe, the good friend and former lover who was the witness at their wedding. Since there were two well-beloved Tough Girls in Toomer's life and only one in *A Drama of the Southwest*, we are also alerted to the possibility that some of the characters of *A Drama of the Southwest* may be composite portraits or representations of what Toomer saw as southwestern types. The play is persistent in its interest in the "strong resourceful women" of the Southwest. As Tom notes:

> You find them in the most unexpected places, here and there over the state, living at the foot of mesas, far removed from everything they have known. And it's they, these women, who are claiming this land which used to be thought of as man's country.[64]

Hanna Gow may thus be a composite of Toomer's own two Tough Girls, Content and O'Keeffe, and contain a little of Luhan and any number of other New Mexico women as well.

MARTHA COLEMAN

If Luhan is in the play, it may be as the holograph's Martha Coleman, a middle-aged woman who appears on Taos Plaza trailed by summer houseguests. Tom Elliot and John Woodward dread running into Martha and joke about losing their balls to her, but Tom pays tribute to her local influence by saying that "to know her is to know Taos."[65] Martha's houseguests, her wealth, and her status as "the grand lady of the place" connect her to Luhan, as does a moment in the holograph when Toomer uses a line of Tom's to indicate a lengthy insertion in the draft, rendering it once as "Have you met Martha?" and once as "Have you meet M.L.?"[66] The initials may be a slip that is suggestive of Mabel Dodge Luhan, but Coleman is not an exact likeness for her. Her "hefty femininity" and "stout body . . . attired in ultra feminine apparel" that is "curiously becoming" make her a better physical representation of Mary Austin, the writer and activist who initially entered the Southwest as a guest of Luhan but eventually set herself up in Santa Fe, where she played host to Willa Cather, among others.[67] The fuller version of *A Drama of the Southwest*, like the artists' community of Taos itself, has no dearth of female strength.

LILLIAN RANGE

It seems likely that Lola Ridge, the radical, Irish-born poet and editor, contributes significantly to the character of Lillian Range. Lillian's "slender, frail-looking body" might belong to almost any tubercular artist, and her medium height is in disaccord with others who remember Ridge as tall, but her "black hair, streaked with gray . . . parted in the middle and pulled down so that, simple, somewhat severe, almost nunlike, it makes an oval frame for her face" is an apt description of the plain but striking woman Marjorie Content captured in photographs of Ridge in 1935.[68] Ridge shares Lillian's initials, also suffers from tuberculosis, and is in New Mexico and headed for Mexico during the summer of 1935, despite the Toomers' fears for her health and their efforts to convince her to stay on. Lola Ridge was, herself, a remarkable figure. The contrast between the frailty of her tuberculosis-wasted body and the strength of her commitment to her ideals captured the imagination of many of her contemporaries. Kay Boyle "cherished her like a small bright flame" and observed that her poetry spoke against social injustice with "a woman's savage voice."[69] Katherine Anne Porter writes of how Ridge put herself in the way of police horses during a 1927 protest in Boston against the execution of Nicola Sacco and Bartolomeo Vanzetti, two working-class anarchists whom many believed innocent of the murders of which they had been convicted:

> One tall, thin figure of a woman stepped out alone, a good distance into the empty square, and when the police came down on her and the horse's hoofs beat over her head, she did not move, but stood with her shoulders slightly bowed, entirely still. The charge was repeated again and again, but she was not to be driven away.[70]

Porter romanticizes the action as the self-sacrifice of an already-doomed woman, stating, "She had not long to live," but Ridge would not succumb to tuberculosis until 1941.[71] If questioned by Porter on the nature of those actions, Ridge might have responded as Lillian does to Tom, when Tom tells her that traveling to Mexico to write in her condition would be suicide. She tells him, "If you do what you need to do, you may meet death, but it is not suicide."[72]

Ridge was a longtime friend of both Toomer and Content. From 1922–1923,

Ridge was the American editor of *Broom*, which had been founded by Content's first husband, Harold Loeb, and had its offices in the basement of Content's brownstone in New York. Toomer was published in *Broom* and attended the salon that Ridge hosted during those years. The year 1935 finds Ridge in Santa Fe, writing the Toomers in Taos to say, "I'd like to see you before I go," an echo of which we hear in Lillian's waiting to see the Elliots in Taos before she travels to Santa Fe and then on to Mexico. In another undated letter, Ridge reports, "I am in a wonderful place that you found for me and it is a boarding house run by a young nurse and her mother."[73] From this letter it seems that Ridge had (at least for a time) taken Content up on an offer that Grace makes to Lillian: "Won't you stay if we find you a better place?"[74] Despite the precariousness of Ridge's health at this point—in addition to grappling with tuberculosis, her letters describe visits to the dentist and a bout with food poisoning—by October of 1936, Ridge is writing the Toomers from Mexico.

Lillian Range in *A Drama of the Southwest* is brave in the face of her illness, but her character lacks Ridge's politics and force. When John Woodward goes to visit her during a fierce rainstorm, he finds her in an adobe house with "water streaming down the walls" and puddling on the floor.[75] Lillian, invalid though she is, is holding an umbrella over her head with one hand and writing poetry with the other. This incident is borrowed from Ridge's life. Ridge writes to her husband in May of 1935 of how the house of a female physician, Dr. Light (rather than the holograph's Dr. Bright and the typescript's Dr. Flanner) in which she was boarding was overwhelmed by rain. "I sat up all night in a chair by the fire in my little room, an umbrella over my head to catch the drips and falling plaster . . . for two days before I left Light's I had to wear golishes [*sic*] in my room."[76]

Lillian is the only artist in the Taos of *A Drama of the Southwest* who is actually producing work, thus escaping the fate that Lola Ridge observed in a letter to Content:

> Taos, place of power and beauty and of the paleface Americans who, like the pigmy cedars upon the mountains, become somehow shrunk and cease to expand beneath the splendor that surrounds them.[77]

Rather than shrink or cease, Lillian Range would write on, even if the skies or the adobe roof fell on her. The play's other artists are more easily derailed.

The First Landlady, Ethel Hart, was once a pianist; Lillian's friend Bill Bryne "wants to write a novel but . . . has to do what the magazines want"; John Woodward writes, paints, and makes furniture (but none of it lately, so caught up is he in his own private drama).[78]

OTHER ARTISTS

It is not clear if the play's other artists are portraits or representations of a general community struggle with artistic frustrations. Toomer's letters of 1934 may provide a hint at some of the basis for the characters of Helen and John Woodward. He touches on the marital troubles of his friends Chaunse Dupee and Tockie Green and his own role in counseling them while he is in Wisconsin. Dupee and Green were both friends from Gurdjieff circles and had been participants in the Portage Experiment, a summer of communal living overseen by Toomer in 1931, and through which Toomer came to know his first wife, Margery Latimer. Like Helen Woodward, Tockie Green came from money and might have faced some parental disapproval in her choice of husband. (Though also the child of a wealthy family, Dupee was once arrested for abandoning and failing to support a previous wife and child while participating in the Portage Experiment.[79]) Toomer's words about Chaunse, "He is in a bad state. . . . Unreasonable, vindictive, distempered, and all the rest"[80] are echoed in Grace's language as she speaks to Helen: "John is in a state. You are in a state. You yourself and John himself are temporarily eclipsed. You can't treat him as if he were his reasonable self. He isn't."[81] The connection between the play and life here exists more in the language of being "in a state" and the role Toomer and Tom both endeavor to play by counseling their friends through relationship troubles than in any real similarity between the Woodwards and the Dupee-Green pairing. There is no indication that Dupee and Green ever joined Toomer and Content in New Mexico, or that suspicions about Green's fidelity plagued Dupee. The connection is a slim one, and here, as elsewhere throughout the play, other readers may see different lives reflected in Toomer's characters. And, whether characters in *A Drama of the Southwest* are wholesale inventions, composite characters, or lightly coded portrayals of members of Toomer's circle (as with Lola Ridge inspiring Lillian Range), together they form a loose portrait of the modernists in Taos and reflect Toomer's own fascination with the desires, dreams, and frustrations of tourists, artists, and neonatives in the Southwest in the early twentieth century.

Notes

1. Stasi, "Synchronous but More Subtle Migration," 148–49. To Stasi's reading, modernism both creates and dismantles racialized discourse. He defines primitivism as "modernist production of blackness" and then locates *Cane*'s modernity in Toomer's use of modernist aesthetics to "question the logic of racialized discourse . . . in the nostalgic primitivism that would seek to discover an 'authentic' blackness in a supposedly premodern South."

2. Members of the Nuevomexicano community, often Catholic and of partly indigenous descent, identify New Mexico as their homeland and trace their families to Spanish or Mexican colonists in the region before its absorption into the United States. Burke, *Greenwich Village to Taos*. Toomer's text, like those of Mabel Dodge Luhan and other Anglo contemporaries, uses "Mexican" as the term for any Hispanic resident of New Mexico.

3. I am indebted to Hal Rothman for the term "neonative," and for his discussion of the growth of tourism and the art scene in Santa Fe and Taos. Rothman defines neonatives as a wave of new residents who are attracted to the "constructed ethos" (and the infrastructures) of tourist towns. These individuals are usually from elite groups of American society and can choose to be underemployed in their newly chosen homeland. They nonetheless tend to capture more of the economic and political benefits of tourism's transformations than do native populations or local residents whose tenure preceded the arrival of the tourists and neonatives. Rothman, *Devil's Bargains*, 21–30.

4. See, e.g., Byrd and Gates, "Jean Toomer's Racial Self-Identification"; Scruggs, "Jean Toomer"; and Turner, "Jean Toomer Exile."

5. Toomer, "Blue Meridian," 650. For the dates on which Toomer worked on the poem, see Kerman and Eldridge, 80.

6. Toomer, "Blue Meridian," 650–51.

7. Ibid., 638.

8. In a statement hand-titled "written for publication a few days before my marriage," Toomer wrote:

There is a new race in America. I am a member of this new race. It is neither white nor black nor in-between. It is the American race, differing as much from white and black as white and black differ from each other. It is possible there are Negro and Indian bloods in my descent along with English, Spanish, Welsh, Scotch, French, Dutch, and German. This is common in America; and it is from all these strains that the American race is being born. But the old divisions into black, white, brown, red are outworn in this country. They have had their day. Now is the time of the birth of a new order, a new vision, a new ideal of man. I proclaim this new order. My marriage to Margery Latimer is the marriage of two Americans.

Published as "A New Race in America," in *Jean Toomer Reader*, ed. Rusch, 105.

9. Margery Latimer to Meridel LeSueur, October 1931. Quoted in Kerman and Eldridge, *Lives of Jean Toomer*, 199.

10. Kerman and Eldridge, *Lives of Jean Toomer*, 80, 200.

11. Ibid., 212.

12. Jean Toomer, Letter to Marjorie Content, July 1, 1934.

13. Emily Lutenski, "A Small Man in Big Spaces," 18–19.

14. Toomer, New Mexico Notebook. Jean Toomer Papers, Box 65, Folder 1482.

15. Toomer, *A Drama of the Southwest*, holograph, 915.65–66.

16. Rudnick, *Utopian Vistas*, 35–36.

17. Jean Toomer, Letter to Marjorie Content, June 15, 1934.

18. The play mentions two distinct plazas, the shop-lined Taos Plaza within the village of Taos, and the plaza at Taos Pueblo, edged by the Rio Pueblo de Taos, the San Geronimo Chapel, and the north house. It is on this latter plaza at Taos Pueblo that scenes 1 and 9 take place.

19. In 1969, Goram Munson reflected on how Toomer's late works "were quite different from *Cane*." Munson writes: "Toomer was no longer drawing the strength of his roots in Negro life and had abandoned his lyrical vein" (quoted in Kerman and Eldridge, *Lives of Jean Toomer*, 390). In the introduction to the 1975 Boni & Liveright edition of *Cane*, Darwin Turner takes up Munson's lament for Toomer's lyricism but locates its loss even earlier, at the moment when Toomer began writing about a "sophisticated urban world" in the second (and last-composed) section of *Cane* (xxiv). See also Turner, "Failure of a Playwright."

20. See Byrd and Gates, "Song of the Son," in *Cane*, xix–lxvi.

21. Toomer, *Drama of the Southwest*, typescript, 917.1.

22. Toomer, *Cane*, 82–83.

23. Toomer, *Drama of the Southwest*, typescript, 917.1.

24. Toomer, *Drama of the Southwest*, holograph, 914.13.

25. Marjorie Content saved newspaper clippings on the struggle for Blue Lake in 1965–1966; how informed she and Toomer may have been of the intricacies of Blue Lake's legal status in 1935 is unclear.

26. Gordon-McCutchan, *Taos Indians*.

27. For a discussion of Toomer's use of dance, see Turner, "Failure of a Playwright."

28. Toomer, *Drama of the Southwest*, typescript, 917.2.

29. Ibid.

30. Ibid.

31. Ibid., 917.3. Ubeam here appropriates a phrase usually applied to the Tibetan Plateau or the Pamir Mountains of central Asia, which may function to mark Taos as possessing high, mountainous beauty to rival that region and as being likewise a site of spiritual pilgrimage. (Toomer would undertake such a journey to India in 1939–1940).

32. Ibid.

33. Ibid., 917.4.

34. Ibid., 917.5.

35. Ibid.

36. Toomer, *Drama of the Southwest*, holograph, 914.26.

37. Ibid.

38. The apparent similarities between Toomer and the main character partly underlie Rudolph P. Byrd's eagerness to classify the play as a "lecture drama." Though Toomer never links the play to that form, Byrd cites Toomer's intent to create such a work, a play that would trap an audience in a theater to be "talked to by an actor as seriously as if this actor were . . . an agent in life through whom certain ideas and feelings of importance are transmitted." Byrd, *Jean Toomer's Years with Gurdjieff*, 131.

39. Toomer, *Drama of the Southwest*, typescript, 917.5.

40. Toomer, *Drama of the Southwest*, holograph, 914.40. The typescript omits the first sentence and reads, "One of those real men—you know the kind I mean—who fancies himself taming shrews and all that." Toomer, *Drama of the Southwest*, typescript, 14.

41. Burke, *Greenwich Village to Taos*, 89–111.

42. Toomer, *Drama of the Southwest*, holograph, 915.65.

43. Deloria, *Playing Indian*, 136–39.

44. Toomer, *Drama of the Southwest*, holograph, 914.43.

45. Ibid., 915.3–4.

46. Also included are "Mexicans," ranchmen, "native whites," summer visitors, and artists. Ibid., 914.64.

47. Ibid.

48. Ibid., 914.11.

49. Kewa Pueblo southwest of Santa Fe was at this time known as Santo Domingo Pueblo.

50. Toomer, *Drama of the Southwest*, holograph, 916.42.

51. Ibid., 914.14.

52. Ibid.

53. Ibid., 914.24.

54. Ibid.

55. Ibid., 914.6, 23.

56. Ibid., 914.9.

57. Ibid., 914.24.

58. Austin's "Cults of the Pueblos" was published in *Century* magazine and reprinted the same year in *Land of Journeys' Ending*. She describes the role of the Pueblo clowns, the Koshare or "Delight-makers" who "keep the community in order with whips of laughter." When creating skits upon "the absurdities of white life," she credits Pueblo performers with "penetration and a power of mimicry that leaves the white observer speechless. As, for instance, when they set the stage for their simple dramas, the presence of a white man is indicated by a pile of tin cans" (33). Austin gestures to the Pueblo ability to critique white culture while building her larger argument in protest of then-ongoing suppression of Pueblo religious and cultural expression, describing this effort as "modernism clos[ing] over the Puebleño" and "filch[ing] from him in the name of education . . . all the most colorful expression of his spiritual experience." (35).

59. Toomer, *Drama of the Southwest*, holograph, 914.25.

60. Byrd, *Jean Toomer's Years with Gurdjieff*, 142.

61. Though this conversation occurs in both the holograph and typescript versions of scene 4, Byrd uses only the typescript in his analysis, and the character names he uses correspond to that draft. He uses Clifford Genth for John Woodward and Lewis Bourne in place of Tom Elliot. See figure 1 in "A Note on the Text."

62. Toomer, *Drama of the Southwest*, holograph, 914.40–41.

63. Jean Toomer, Letters to Marjorie Content, June 7 and 10, 1934.

64. Toomer, *Drama of the Southwest*, typescript, 917.30.

65. Toomer, *Drama of the Southwest*, holograph, 916.46.

66. Ibid., 916.34, 916.46.

67. Ibid., 914.73.

68. Ibid., 914.27.

69. Kay Boyle is quoted in Tobin, "Modernism, Leftism, and the Spirit," xiii.

70. Porter, *Never-Ending Wrong*, 43–44.

71. Ibid., 44.

72. Toomer, *Drama of the Southwest*, holograph, 916.45.

73. Lola Ridge, Letter to Marjorie Content, 1935.

74. Toomer, *Drama of the Southwest*, holograph, 916.44.

75. Toomer, *Drama of the Southwest*, typescript, 917.28.

76. Lola Ridge, Letter to David Lawson, May 1935.

77. Lola Ridge, Letter to Marjorie Content, undated.

78. Toomer, *Drama of the Southwest*, holograph, 916.32

79. "Register of the Atwood, Ormsby, and Green family papers, 1853–1998."

80. Jean Toomer, Letter to Marjorie Content, June 10, 1934.

81. Toomer, *Drama of the Southwest*, holograph, 916.108.

A Note on the Text

This edition of *A Drama of the Southwest* is a hybrid of two surviving but partial drafts. These are a 57-page typescript of four scenes and a 270-page handwritten manuscript of ten scenes. Those few stray pages that do not fit within the assembled play are included in the appendices, along with the nearly complete holograph version of scene 4. I have left Toomer's language as I found it, including his frequent use of "which" in restrictive clauses. Square brackets indicate insertions or substitutions for obvious errors, and in the latter case, footnotes provide the original language. Where possible, this edition has favored the names used in the longer holograph draft.

The typescript of *A Drama of the Southwest* opens with a night scene at Taos Pueblo, proceeds through a philosophical dialogue on a rooftop to a brief speech by a chorus-like figure, the Interpreter, and ends with an extended scene of the arrival of Lewis and Grace Bourne in Taos. The arrival scene opens at least two plot arcs that are never concluded in this draft—reported trouble in the marriage of the Bournes' friend, Clifford Genth, and the couple's search for belonging in Taos, as expressed through their desire to buy land and through their interactions with other visitors and neonatives. Though some scholars have treated these four scenes as a complete but inconclusive one-act play, attention to the holograph draft reveals them to be only the beginning of a larger work.

The holograph draft contains a mostly complete version of the arrival scene—the only scene duplicated between these two drafts—but the rest of its material is unique. All that follows—two more days of action including Tom Elliot's donkey-interrupted attempts to write, his interference with the Woodward marriage, the Taos Plaza scene and the final evening at the

FIGURE 1. NAMES

This table provides the names used in the typescript and holograph drafts. Speech prefixes used in this edition are bolded. Additional names provided in context in the play are supplied parenthetically.

Typescript	*Holograph*
Ubeam Riseling	Taos Visionary
Buck Fact (Buckter T. Fact)	Taos Kid
Interpreter	
Lewis Bourne	Tom **Elliot**
Grace Bourne	**Grace** Elliot
Betty Bourne	**Betty** Elliot
First Landlady (Ethel Hart)	First Landlady (Edith)
Second Landlady (Lucy)	**Second Landlady** (Mary)
Hanna Gow	Tough Girl (Lucy Frisk)
	Martha Coleman
Clifford Genth (Clif)	**John** Woodward
Helen Genth	**Helen** Woodward
	Mrs. Ogline
Riva Lentin	**Lillian** Range
	Bill **Bryne**
	Vincent Weir

FIGURE 2. SCENES

This chart displays the limited overlap of the holograph and typescript drafts of *A Drama of the Southwest.* The holograph version of scene 4 is slightly incomplete and is included as Appendix A.

	Typescript	*Holograph*
1	Taos Pueblo at night.	
2	Rooftop dialog of Ubeam Riseling and Buckter T. Fact.	
3	Speech by the Interpreter.	
4	House with roofers working above. Landladies are joined by Hanna Gow; Lewis Bourne and Grace Bourne arrive; Clifford Genth arrives. Lewis describes their trip; Lewis and Clifford discuss Clifford's marital problems and the	Tough Girl talks to the Landladies, roofers above. Tom Elliot and Grace Elliot arrive. John Woodward and Tom Elliot discuss Bournes' plan to buy land. John Woodward and Tom Elliot discuss John's marital problems and the Elliots' plan to buy land.

(Scenes continued)

5	The Elliots' bedroom, 9:00 p.m. Tom and Grace Elliot discuss the trip; spiders; Pueblo Indians go by outside, singing.
6	Rooftop dialogue, Taos Visionary and Taos Kid.
7	Morning. Tom Elliot dances. Grace Elliot goes to town; Tom writes with interruptions. He reads Grace the letter on her return.
8	Lillian Range and Bill Bryne arrive at the Elliots' home for tea. The four discuss Taos, Blue Lake, and Martha Coleman; Lillian and Bill agree to stay for dinner and a trip to the Pueblo.
9	Taos Pueblo at night with Grace and Tom Elliot, Lillian Range, and Bill Bryne.
10	Rooftop dialogue, Taos Visionary and Taos Kid.
11	Taos Plaza, 10 a.m., with various populations of Taos represented. Landladies tell Tough Girl about Tom Elliot's dancing; Bill Bryne flees Martha Coleman and runs into Tom. Tom and Martha exchange barbs.
12	Grace Elliot and Helen Woodward discuss Helen's rumored affair. Tom Elliot arrives and confronts Helen's mother, Mrs. Ogline.
13	4:30 p.m. Grace and Tom discuss the Woodwards. Vincent Weir visits with news of the land. Lillian Range and Frank Milner arrive for tea.

pueblo—is unique to the holograph. The thematic and chronological reach of the incomplete *A Drama of the Southwest* is far greater than that of the typescript.

The four scenes in the typescript survive in the archive in neatly numbered pages. The pages are in order and none are missing. The practice of assuming the completeness of this typed draft and ignoring the more extensive holograph draft has functioned as an editorial process, even if an inadvertent one, because it implies a belief that Toomer abandoned it, slashing a lively and ambitious full-length drama into a complete one-act play of significantly smaller ambition. But even if it could be proved that Toomer revised *A Drama of the Southwest* in this ill-advised manner, there would be no reason to be over-punctilious about final or authoritative drafts. There is little evidence that the holograph draft is a rough or abandoned version of the typescript. The play's archive provides evidence of Toomer alternating between typewriting and handwriting as he composes, and thus cautions against imagining a simple hierarchy in which typed drafts replace and supersede holograph ones. Indeed, the holograph draft contains a single stray typewritten page that uses character names that match the holograph draft instead of the typescript, and which is type-numbered 116.[1] If this page was truly once the 116th page of a draft about the Elliots, it is therefore likely that the draft I have been referring to as the holograph once boasted a mass of typed material twice as large as that of the four-scene "typescript." It is partly as a gesture to the weight of those lost pages that this edition favors the character names from the holograph.

A Drama of the Southwest as printed here has a few obvious gaps: part of scene 11 on Taos Plaza, the end of scene 13 and any action that may have followed it, and parts of the holograph scene 4 in appendix A. But there are moments in which the archive gestures to still larger absences. The pair of fragments in appendix B seem to belong to some dialogue between Tom Elliot and Clifford Genth, perhaps also in scene 4. Appendix C contains a manifesto-like paragraph that appears in neither extant draft, but which Toomer attributes parenthetically as "taken from Drama of the Southwest." If this text is indeed excerpted from *A Drama of the Southwest*, it comes from some part of a draft of the play now unavailable: perhaps one of those missing 115 typed pages. The choice to consider *A Drama of the Southwest* in its surviving entirety is one that invites some degree of imagination for what is unrecoverable.

Toomer did not number his holograph scenes, so the order of the scenes here is assembled from hints in the play's internal chronology, and they are numbered for convenience only. Some placements are more tenuous than others. In the spirit of expansive inclusion of text, this edition begins each of the three days with a rooftop dialog between the Taos Visionary, Ubeam Riseling, and the Taos Kid, Buckter T. Fact. These scenes might as easily be viewed as versions, possible substitutions for the dialogue in scene 2 instead of as scenes to be placed at the outset of each day. Such reorganizations (and perhaps even more daring ones) are for the readers and users of this text to undertake. Compression and rearrangements would also be warranted should one view the play's two stagings of the Elliot family's journey to New Mexico—in dialogue with John Woodward in scene 4 and in epistolary recitation in scene 7—as versions rather than iterations.

This edition ends at teatime on the third day with Grace Elliot opening her door to Lillian Range and the Communist Frank Milner. The ensuing scene and the play's original or projected denouement are, quite obviously, absent from the surviving pages. With minimal alteration of internal references, a more formally satisfying (and perhaps more playable) draft of *A Drama of the Southwest* could readily be created by ordering the scenes 1–7, 11–13, 8–9. It was this ordering—and a two-day chronology—I favored in my article, "Jean Toomer, Sojourner."[2] Such a draft would open and close the play at Taos Pueblo and end with Tom Elliot's line, "Indians of pueblo, you will not hear me, but thank you—and goodnight" rather than Grace Elliot's "Someone is coming."[3] Whether arranged to offer the expansive possibilities of the unfinished in which "someone is coming," or to offer the closure of Tom's, "goodnight," it is my hope that *A Drama of the Southwest* offers a Jean Toomer and a Southwest not yet fully known to us, a text in which we, too, may strike rich and new experience.

Notes

1. Toomer, *Drama of the Southwest*, holograph, 916.101. This page begins the second surviving portion of scene 11 on Taos Plaza. The first three lines are typed, and then Toomer fills the rest of the page by hand and continues the conversation between Tom Elliot and Bill Bryne on subsequent handwritten pages.

2. Dekker, "Jean Toomer, Sojourner." The Taos Plaza scene, here scene 11, is the most difficult to place. The landladies report upon Elliot's dancing (scene 7) as if they have just finished settling their tenants, implying proper placement shortly after that scene on the morning of the second day. However, Bill Bryne soon apologizes to Hanna Gow for having stood her up because he was with the Elliots and Lillian Range the night before, implying that this scene comes on a third day, or at least after the second night scene at Taos Pueblo (here scene 9).

3. Toomer, *Drama of the Southwest*, holograph, 916.24.

Dramatis Personae

ELLIOT: Tom Elliot, a writer, philosopher, and New York intellectual summering in Taos and seeking to buy land.

GRACE: Grace Elliot, wife of Tom, a more experienced Taoseña.

BETTY: Their daughter.

UBEAM: Mr. Ubeam Riseling, poet, import, visionary.

BUCK FACT: Buckter T. Fact, butcher, proletarian, plazaboy.

INTERPRETER

FIRST LANDLADY: Ethel Hart, a former concert pianist who raised her children in Taos after injury forced her to give up the stage.

SECOND LANDLADY: Mary.

HANNA: Hanna Gow, the "Tough Girl," a year-round resident of Taos.

JOHN: John Woodward, the Elliots' friend, a painter who is not painting.

HELEN: Helen Woodward, wife of John, who believes her to have been unfaithful.

MRS. OGLINE: Helen's mother.

LILLIAN: Lillian Range, a New York poet who suffers from tuberculosis.

BRYNE: Bill Bryne, Lillian's friend; romantic interest of Hanna Gow.

INDIAN: An older man from Taos Pueblo.

MARTHA: Martha Coleman, the wealthy patroness who collects houseguests in Taos.

VIN: Vincent Weir, editor of the *Taos Valley News*.

FRANK MILNER: The Communist.

A Drama of the Southwest

1

Night-black, night of the New Mexican Southwest, a luminous black sky, and the stars seem close to Earth. Into this sky of quiet ecstasy the form of a mountain lifts. The mountain, vast itself, lifts into the greater immensity of the universe as manifest at this viewpoint. The surrounding hills repose beneath the intensity of stars.

The line of the slope is broken by a gap—a canyon to the country north.

This side of the mountain, fitted into its slope, are the two terraced forms of Taos Pueblo, one on each side of the creek that comes down from Blue Lake.

On a high terrace of each pueblo building is the figure of an Indian, robed in white, face to the hills.

No lights show from the houses. No figures cross the plaza. No dogs bark. The only sounds are those made by the creek as it runs its course from Taos Mountain to the Rio Grande.

The night, the mountain, the pueblo, the silent men—all seem simply to have come into being . . . being by birth . . . created but not labored—the night from all preceding nights, the mountain from the ample earth, the pueblo from all dwellings back to the cliffs, the men from all the people of their race.

It is quiet. In this silence, repose and intensity coexist. Then comes a call, human, but like a high bark. Several robed figures emerge from the houses, pass across the plaza, and exchange greetings—"Hé-ah-ho." The voices are those of men.

The men gather at a bridge over the stream.

Pause, silence.

Then suddenly a Taos song. Another song and another.

Then silence again . . . and life becomes existence again . . . and existence, focused for a time in a group of singing men, expands to the mountain and the close stars.

2

Day of the Southwest, a brilliant blue sky in a vast arch, sun, intense dry heat.

An adobe house of which chiefly the roof is seen. Against one side of the house a weathered cedar ladder slants, its two poles rising somewhat higher than the roof. On this roof is a chair. In this chair sits a figure wrapped in a blanket like an Indian, though he is not an Indian. He is Mr. Ubeam Riseling, poet, import, and visionary, a person of some depth and dignity who does not belong to the art colony because he is above art. Directly opposite Ubeam a second figure is also on the roof *but not in a chair. This second figure, wearing blue jeans soft and pale from many washings, lies nonchalantly, propped on an elbow, absently plucking and chewing bits of roof grass. He is* Mr. Buckter T. Fact, *butcher, proletarian, and plazaboy, a realistic person of some intelligence who does not belong to the art colony because he is below art. The two figures face each other, but whereas the visionary gazes off into space, the realist sizes the visionary up.*

UBEAM: *(speaking from himself to the wide world, inadvertently or in any case only incidentally including* Buck Fact*)* This is the roof of the world.

BUCK FACT: *(now using his other elbow for support)* Is it!

UBEAM: Thy house, O earth, is of adobe, mixed through the geologic ages and baked by the everlasting sun. From far up the canyon where the great trees are, the vigas* came—and who was the builder?

BUCK FACT: A house, a roof, you say? The roof of the world? Elevation six thousand nine hundred odd feet. Over Raton Pass . . . down Cimarron Canyon . . . curve by Eagle Nest Lake . . . sweep down Moreno Valley . . . then cross a pass or two, and you too, my dear tourists, will be here on the roof of the world, even as he and I.

UBEAM: There are two aspects of mystery. On one side you will find the mysterious, on the other you will find the queer.

BUCK FACT: I'll vouch for the queer. The longer I live the more queer people I see, and I do believe that everyone is queer save thou and me, and as for thee. . . . As for Taos—go down to the plaza any day and you'll sight more queer birds per square yard than you'll find anywhere else on this adobe planet.

UBEAM: Back by the mountain where the stream comes down, tumbling twenty miles from Blue Lake, is Taos Pueblo, the most beautiful of all. Its people do not know their own history, nor do we.

BUCK FACT: Nearby, however, lives a writer who sees to it that her history is better known.

UBEAM: The spirit of the Indian still lives in and dominates this land. Disappearing elsewhere, it is vital here, vital like these hills, living since Jicarilla

* Vigas are rough-hewn roof beams that are characteristic of adobe architecture even in ancient cliff dwellings. Beginning in the 1920s and '30s, ornamental vigas were incorporated into New Mexico public architecture.

was a volcano. Indians of the pueblo, you have charmed these mountains, you have filled the canyons with echoes, you have magnetized Taos. To this little cluster of earth-built houses the entire world comes.

BUCK FACT: Comes and goes as fast as it can. It is amazing, though, the way they come. License plates from every state in the Union, from Canada, and even from Europe, too. And why? What's to be seen here? One bank, one newspaper, grocery and drug stores like you can see anywhere, an armory, a baseball field, a fish hatchery, bad roads, the plaza, and a dump heap. Why should anyone come all this way to get dust in his eyes? As for me, it means a job. I'm the butcher at McNulty's.

UBEAM: One of the laws of the cosmos is to the effect that a reciprocality must be established: That which draws in must also give out. Taos magnetizes, hence it must create. In the days of the great seasons, after this awful winter of man, something very great will come to growth in the Southwest, uniting the geography and the people, the earth and mankind, this planet and the universe. Remember that the cactus blooms.

3

INTERPRETER: People are coming, people from the East. They will find this land preinhabited, even as the first desert was; but they will come as if discovering Taos, planting their flag in this high earth. They will come southwestward, not on horseback or in a covered wagon but driving a motorcar. Even so they will strike experience here, as man ever does when his heart is freshly given to a place. First the Indians came. Then the Spaniards. Then the fair-skinned northern folk. So, in their turn, our man and woman come, moving in the restlessness of peoples—two people in search of their environment, two human beings seeking an answer to the question: "What is my function in life?"

4

Taos. 4 p.m. a June afternoon. Interior of an adobe house. One room, a combined studio, bedroom, and living room. It is equipped with studio bed, Mexican chairs, two nondescript tables, electric lamps, and a sort of wardrobe closet. The floor is of earth. In one corner is a fireplace, southwestern. Several pieces of piñon wood are in a basket nearby. Above this basket is a bookshelf. One door opens into the yard. The other connects with the second room of the house. A large double window gives a view of Taos Mountain.

Two women, the landladies of the place, are busy fixing up in anticipation of the arrival of summer tenants. The First Landlady, *taller and leaner than the other, is in blue jeans and a blue work shirt, and has a dark red scarf around her head. The* Second Landlady *is in corduroy trousers and a blue work shirt, and her hair with its man-style cut is creased at the back from wearing a Stetson hat. There is a third woman helping, a Mexican of short stature and ample female figure. She is putting tierra blanca on the walls and passes in and out. Except for their hips and the fact that they call each other "dear," the two women might at first glance be mistaken for men.*

Workmen are repairing the roof damaged by storms. From the roof come sounds of pounding. At each thud, particles of adobe mud fall from the ceiling. After each shower, the women make haste to clean up. The men on the roof pass from spot to spot. The women on the floor likewise pass from spot to spot.

SECOND LANDLADY: I do hope they won't arrive today. A house is a mess when tenants leave it, but I still cling to my code that it should be clean when they take it.

FIRST LANDLADY: You shouldn't say hope. You hope for what you want. You don't hope for what you don't want.

SECOND LANDLADY: You should know what I mean.

FIRST LANDLADY: You should say what you mean.

SECOND LANDLADY: I mean I'd like to know exactly where they are and exactly when they will arrive. Suspense is all right in novels.

FIRST LANDLADY: Their letter was posted in Denver. They said they'd arrive tomorrow. If they got our letter before they left New York they know the storms we've had and they know the house was damaged and they must realize that torrents are torrents and mud is mud, even if it is called adobe.

SECOND LANDLADY: That was two weeks ago. In two weeks in the East they'd put up a skyscraper.

FIRST LANDLADY: That may be. This is New Mexico. I sometimes wish we didn't have this place. Something is always happening to it. If it isn't the roof it's the wall, if it isn't the wall it's the windows, if it isn't the windows—

SECOND LANDLADY: Didn't have it? What would we do?

FIRST LANDLADY: I've never found time weighing on my hands. Leave a career as I did, come out here and bring up three children—and after all that I'd like to look forward to a little leisure.

SECOND LANDLADY: Ethel dear, we forgot to get that ironing board.

FIRST LANDLADY: We did. They won't use it. Have you the key to the *escusado?*

SECOND LANDLADY: You need it?

FIRST LANDLADY: I want it. I wonder if they'll like this place when they see it.

SECOND LANDLADY: She's seen it. Why do you think she got in touch with us? I don't know about him. Writers are fussy.

FIRST LANDLADY: Stop talking about writers. You can thank your stars he is. If he were a businessman they'd have taken a house in Santa Fe where he could go on being civilized with telephones—not that I want them.

SECOND LANDLADY: I'm not talking about writers, or painters either. I could, though. Stop talking about Santa Fe. Here's the key.

FIRST LANDLADY: I don't want it. I simply wanted to know where it was.

SECOND LANDLADY: Anything else you want?

FIRST LANDLADY: You needn't be sarcastic. Hand me that dustpan. (*She looks up at the ceiling.*) Won't they ever finish? My back aches.

SECOND LANDLADY: All right, your back aches.

Someone on the outside calls hello. Both Landladies *give a start and regard each other with consternation.*

SECOND LANDLADY: Elliots?

FIRST LANDLADY: Don't stand there. Go see who it is.

Enter Hanna Gow. Hanna Gow *is a slender, mannish woman of about the same age as the* Landladies. *She is handsome. Her face is finely modeled, with sensitive nostrils. Life has hurt her. Her chin has become aggressive, her manner casual and hardboiled. A woman of peculiar pallor and thin red lips. Her outfit is a pair of cowboy boots, blue jeans, blue shirt, and a Spanish-style black felt hat which she swings in her hand.*

The Landladies *greet her, then resume sweeping up the mud that continues to drop as the men on the roof heave away at their steady unremitting tamping.*

HANNA GOW: Not finished yet?

FIRST LANDLADY: Oh! It's you!

HANNA GOW: Who did you think it was? Didn't you hear the horse? I'm riding this afternoon.

SECOND LANDLADY: We thought it was the Elliots.

HANNA GOW: Don't make that mistake again. I'm not Grace Elliot and I never expect to be. How much longer is it going to take?

FIRST LANDLADY: The men promised to be finished today, but you know how it is. Took a week to get them to start work; now I suppose it will take a week to get them to stop. They really aren't finished. I hope this job will be the last for this summer.

HANNA GOW: Then why don't you wait? What's the use of trying to clean when the stuff keeps falling down?

FIRST LANDLADY: We never thought of that.

SECOND LANDLADY: Yes we did, but what are we to do? They may arrive any minute. How'd you like to find your place a mess after coming all the way from New York? Besides, we've varnished the kitchen floor and don't want dirt tracked in. If they come today they'll have to stay at the Inn.*

HANNA GOW: Why not? They can afford it. Let them be thankful they weren't here when we all got washed out. You're becoming slaves to this mud house. Don't take so much on yourself. I hate her.

SECOND LANDLADY: We know you do. Why?

HANNA GOW: The way she dresses when she gets out here. Ugh!

SECOND LANDLADY: Nothing wrong that I can see, except that she does wear dresses.

HANNA GOW: Now what do you mean by that?

SECOND LANDLADY: Just what I say.

* Throughout the holograph and typescript, Toomer capitalizes "Inn," as if his characters have a specific establishment in mind. The Taos Inn, however, did not open until 1936, and did so under the name of Hotel Martin. The Sagebrush Inn is an even more venerable Taos lodging and is another possible candidate. Though it first went by the name of El Chamiso Lodge when it was built in 1930–1931, it was also sometimes referred to as a "wayside inn." In a May 1935 letter to her husband, Lola Ridge described being flooded out of her lodgings and taking refuge "at wayside inn," probably meaning El Chamiso—the Sagebrush Inn.

FIRST LANDLADY: Then you mean too much. Are we or aren't we going to finish cleaning this floor?

HANNA GOW: I'm not fond of him, either. One of those real men men—you know the kind I mean, who fancies himself taming shrews and all that. The damn conceited fool. Don't wish them any bad luck, but I hope they both get drowned in the floods. Which way are they coming?

FIRST LANDLADY: The Conoco man said Kansas can't be crossed.

SECOND LANDLADY: Colorado isn't much better.

HANNA GOW: Here's hoping. What are they coming to Taos for, anyway? No one wants them.

BOTH LANDLADIES: We do.

HANNA GOW: Of course. I'd welcome Jesus Christ if he'd rent my house.

A car is heard to stop on the road before the house. It starts again and seems to be going around to the garage. Both Landladies *jump.*

BOTH LANDLADIES: Them?

HANNA GOW: *(making a face)* We'll see soon enough.

Exit two Landladies *in a flutter.* Hanna Gow *starts to make her exit out the side door, then reconsiders. She remains in the room, eyes lowered, swinging her hat, uneasy and angry that she may be caught in the situation of the Elliots' arrival. Hellos and greetings are heard outside.* Tom Elliot *enters, bent on seeing the house. Elliot is a tall man of forty, critical, disposed to be sociable in manner while his eyes look on. His body is somewhat stooped, as if all his life he has had to bend down to get through doors too low for him. He wears grey flannel trousers, Norfolk coat, blue shirt with soft collar. He is surprised to see* Hanna Gow *standing in the room, yet greets her by name cordially, as she is part of the New Mexico to which he has just arrived with fresh enthusiasm.* Hanna *says hello but does not unbend. Elliot then glances around the room, appraising it to discover if he is going to like living in it. His eyes fasten on the ceiling. He is about to make some comment on the pounding and the falling particles of mud when—*

HANNA GOW: Well, how are men? I suppose you've started the revolution?

ELLIOT: Men? Oh, men. Exactly what your opinion of them is.

HANNA GOW: They are marvels, then. What about the revolution?

ELLIOT: Which revolution?

HANNA GOW: The one you are going to start against female Fascism.

Elliot. Still underground.

HANNA GOW: Your name is known.

ELLIOT: I'm aware of it. I fully expect to be put in a concentration camp in Taos before the summer is over. Will you see to it?

HANNA GOW: Gladly.

ELLIOT: So pleased you are here to welcome me. If you can't make friends, make enemies.

Enter Grace Elliot *with the* Landladies.

Grace Elliot, *younger than her husband, is a splendid woman-type, dark hair, dark eyes, natural and open in manner, with a joy in moving her body. She is dressed in a striped grey sport suit. Happy to have arrived, she accepts the house, accepts the room, the mud, the men tamping, even accepts* Hanna Gow *though she is aware that Hanna and herself are not supposed to like each other.*

FIRST LANDLADY: We're so sorry we aren't ready for you, but your letter said you'd arrive tomorrow.

GRACE: We didn't know what we'd strike south of Denver. You know about the floods. Colorado Springs was a wreck. I've never seen anything like it. The mud was simply awful.

FIRST LANDLADY: So it was here. We had torrents, seven days and seven nights—almost biblical. The house was left in a frightful mess, as I wrote you. Did you get our last letter? The roof leaked, the walls were stained. Some of your rugs and pillow covers are still in Santa Fe being cleaned. We hoped to have everything done, but the men are working on the roof and we've been cleaning up after them all day.

GRACE: We'll make out.

FIRST LANDLADY: I hope you won't mind staying at the Inn tonight.

GRACE: The Inn? No thank you. We've been living in inns and hotels and camps for two weeks. We want to unpack and get settled.

FIRST LANDLADY: But the men will be working tomorrow too.

GRACE: We won't mind that. We want to get settled.

FIRST LANDLADY: Your laundry isn't here. There's not a sheet or a towel in the house. It's ready, but we haven't had time to call for it. The place closes at five.

GRACE: Tom, what time is it?

ELLIOT: Five of five.

GRACE: I'm going for the laundry. Will you bring the suitcases in? I know where the laundry is.

SECOND LANDLADY: All the roads are torn up.

GRACE: I'll find my way. We promised ourselves we'd sleep in our own place tonight.

SECOND LANDLADY: Where's your little girl?

GRACE: Playing outside. I'll take her with me. Goodbye.

Exit Grace. *Soon after she has gone,* Hanna Gow *moves to the door and goes out without saying a word.* Elliot *follows her departure with his eyes and shakes his head.*

FIRST LANDLADY: (*to* Elliot) I'm so afraid you won't be comfortable here tonight, and we do want you to like our little house. (*looks up at the ceiling*) Well, thank goodness, they're going over the other room. I'll just clean up and you won't track it through.

She sweeps again. She finishes.

FIRST LANDLADY: Mary, what are you doing standing there in a daze? Get your broom and come with me. Mr. Elliot, if you'll wait just a minute before getting your bags, we'll have a path swept in the next room and you won't track dirt through.

Both Landladies *go out, closing the door behind them.* Elliot *smiles, shrugs, lights a cigarette, and goes to the window from which can be seen the dark form of Taos Mountain, a nest of white clouds, and the blue-brilliant sky of a New Mexican late afternoon. Presently he leaves the room, soon to return with suitcases, which he stacks in a corner. This finished, he tries to fit into a creaking Mexican armchair. He gets to his feet, fishes in a duffle bag, and produces a bottle of whisky. There is a knock on the door leading from the room to the yard outside.* Elliot *goes and opens it and greets* John Woodward.

John Woodward, *as tall as* Elliot, *is heavy boned and seems always to have something weighing on him. He is both proud and apologetic, genial and embittered, easygoing and tempestuous. He smokes a pipe, wears glasses, and makes a point of appearing in conventional city clothes.*

ELLIOT: Well, John! Glad to see you. Come right in.

JOHN: Heard you were arriving. Came out on a chance. How're things? How're Grace and the baby? Have a good trip?

Elliot *closes both doors.* John *stands around as if he may not be welcome, as if someone may jump on him.*

ELLIOT: Quite a voyage, in fact, with dangers of a kind and a lively sense of the unknown. To cross the earth was adventure this time, yet not pleasant to be reminded of our puppet-place. In our new Ford we were like ants, zigzagging to escape cloudbursts, floods, washouts, and the general compulsion toward catastrophe. Nature, it would seem, has come to her final protest against us who, having power, are less than we should be. She would rid herself of our rapacious arrogance, even if this means the end of man as the dominant species. Has it struck you, John, that there seems to be a concerted attempt, not far scattered episodes but a unified upheaval, as if the very planet itself were fighting off a sickness, as if each acre, remembering all the wrong done it, were discontent—

JOHN: I'm afraid I can't answer for the earth. Haven't been out of Taos for two years. Don't want to go. I'll take what's coming to me here. There's enough and to spare. At least I know the compulsion toward catastrophe, as you put it. Sometimes I'm afraid I can't even answer for myself.

ELLIOT: Something particularly wrong? I, you will note, am characteristic of my time in that I'm interested only in the grave great troubles. The lesser ills must go by the boards.

JOHN: I'll be able to interest you.

ELLIOT: What is it? Helen and you, or just yourself, or you and Taos? Or have you, too, suddenly been struck to realize the diabolical insanity of poverty in the midst of plenty and you want to know what to do about it?

JOHN: I'd like to talk, but not now. You've just arrived. The women will be barging in. Christ, it's good you've come. Jesus Christ, it's good to talk with a man—any man, but you especially. We'll go off by ourselves, sometime soon.

ELLIOT: Righto. Sounds as if you've been on a fast.

JOHN: Sounds as if! You left here the tenth of last September. From that day to this there hasn't, as we may say, there hasn't been a man in my life.

ELLIOT: That is serious.

JOHN: More than you feel, you who live in New York where things are going on and men and women live in something like a balance, you who have Grace and no damn in-laws to rub it in that you aren't worthy of their daughter. You know Helen's mother came on?

ELLIOT: How could I know? You haven't written. What is this hole you've dug for yourself? What do you call it? What way is the resurrection of John Woodward, man, human being, and my friend?

JOHN: *(passing a hand over his face)* What way. Do you know a way? That isn't what I was talking about. What was I talking about? Oh, her. She came on. Now her permanent residence is beside her daughter in the casa de Woodward. Always says she's going, never goes. Says she hates Taos and loves the East. Says too goddamn much. So you see how it is. If I stay home I have her delightful company. If I go out, I run into the incorporated females of Taos.

ELLIOT: What a plight, women to right of you, women to left of you—and your only choice is to up or down. You're a tragic man, John.

JOHN: I'm tragedy itself. It isn't the women who need men, it's the *men* who need men. A hell of a setup. And now, dammit, if I come out to see you I'll run into your charming landladies.

ELLIOT: How so?

JOHN: You'll come to know the dears. Ever hear them dearing each other? Guess not. That was in vogue last year. This year they're bitching each other. Relationships do change, even the best. What I was going to say is this: Ever see meticulous possessiveness personified? That's them. They've been working on this house two solid weeks—a three-room house, two husky women—and I'll bet it isn't finished yet. They never finish. They'll pop in and out all summer, tinkering with this, puttering with that. It's yours in theory, it won't be yours in fact.

ELLIOT: In any event it's mine for the moment, and you are welcome, so sit down and we'll drink to—what?

JOHN: There you have it. We don't even know what to drink to any more.

John *nevertheless unbends. The two of them take chairs at the table.* Elliot *pours drinks.*

ELLIOT: Oh well, we'll find something.

JOHN: Aren't they likely to barge in?

ELLIOT: Here's how. No, I don't think so. Our masculine privacy is insured for the time by the simple fact that they do not want dirt tracked through. Dirt, you see, has its advantages. When we arrived this afternoon the ladies were in the throes of cleaning up the adobe droppings that fell from our too generous ceiling. The said ladies were stitched and dithered lest Grace and I, particularly I, track dirt. It is still reasonable to assume—

JOHN: What did I tell you? All summer they'll be stitched and dithered lest one thing or another—and no one damn thing of any consequence. That's what gripes me. If the fuss were about something—but no. They'd go about meticulously with dustpan and brush—

ELLIOT: I get the picture perfectly. Have a cigarette?

JOHN: I'm serious, Tom. What in hell has happened? How did life slip from the control of men? Why is it a woman's world? What's the matter with our women? Indian women aren't like this. Our women weren't this way a century ago. You pick up a book or a magazine and all you read about is the economic problem. The economic problem is nothing compared to the problem between men and women.

ELLIOT: Now it's my turn to be afraid. I'm afraid, John, that I understand little or nothing about causes. I have a somewhat better understanding of cures—strange though such a statement may seem. About the world, I don't know. About some individuals I do know a little something, perhaps a serviceable something. Someday when you are in the mood for it, ask me how life slipped from your control, ask me why you haven't a world, ask me what's the matter with you—and we may be able to work out something.

JOHN: As you wish.

ELLIOT: Tell me about our landladies. How long have they been as we see them now?

JOHN: Them? Oh, it started about a year ago. Before that, they were sensible women with heads on their shoulders, hard working, admirable in every particular. Then suddenly they were struck by that curious disaffection called female-itus. Overnight they became fussy and jittery about the house, about everything. It was as if some hope, some future went to sleep or died in them. It was exactly as if they had lost their heads and their nerves moved their bodies about senselessly. The way they went at it you would have thought they wanted to fuss themselves into utter exhaustion.

ELLIOT: A most curious disaffection. Any idea what happened?

JOHN: I have my guesses. They're in their forties. Queer things are said to happen to women then. Everybody in Taos guessed—and some of our good citizens, as is their custom, did more than guess.

ELLIOT: You don't mean they talked?

JOHN: That kind of talk is called gossip.

ELLIOT: They actually gossiped?

JOHN: Joke about it if you want, but wait until it hits you.

ELLIOT: God forbid.

JOHN: Quite beyond His power.

ELLIOT: What exactly is the relationship between landlady one and landlady two?

JOHN: That's one of those questions you ask but don't answer. Can't tell you. I've seen them together long enough to accept them without asking. You've heard the story of Ethel Hart? She's no ordinary person, she.

ELLIOT: What is the story?

JOHN: Well, she lived in New York, was a concert pianist with a career. Then the skies fell. She injured her hand and had to give up piano. Her husband died and left her with two children* and no money. She came out here on a shoestring. God knows how she's done it. Somehow, she scraped together enough money to buy a second house, which is considerably more than I've done. She's brought up those children, exceptional children. She's been through hell, and nobody has ever heard a whimper from her. Maybe what's happened to her now is the strain of all those years finally breaking through. Or, is it simply that she has lived too long in Taos, that what was effort is now inertia, and that the inertia has turned hysterical?

* The First Landlady, Ethel Hart, herself refers to raising three children.

ELLIOT: It may be. There's an interesting thing about the Southwest. It attracts an unusual kind of woman—strong resourceful women who like the starkness and isolation of this country and have the power to be alone. You find them in the most unexpected places, here and there over the state, living at the foot of mesas, far removed from everything they have known. And it's they, these women, who are claiming this land which used to be thought of as man's country. But to return to what you asked—I know this in general. Fussiness is a symptom of underuse. Inertia is a flow without a goal. If you have nothing important to live for you are consumed by the unimportant. As a substitute for big issues you make issues of trifles. If not to the stars, your weight and force become attached to mud. How old are her children?

JOHN: Old enough to take care of themselves.

ELLIOT: What else does she do now besides keeping this house in disorder?

JOHN: Not much, any more. The same can be said of more than one of us in Taos. I wouldn't deny the accusation that the reason we're here is because we're in ruts and want to stay in them. Let the world change all it wants; we'll remain as we are.

ELLIOT: Weren't you all but washed out several weeks ago?

JOHN: You talk about ants. Three weeks ago today the skies fell. They fell for a solid week. For a time it looked as if there would be nothing left but streams of mud. Even at the pueblo some of the houses leaked and the Indians camped in the school buildings, and for once the government buildings were put to unquestionably good use. The funniest sight was Lillian Range.

ELLIOT: How is she?

JOHN: Quite well when I last saw her, much improved despite the torrents. She was waiting for you and Grace to come. You know how otherworldly Lillian is, much here mentally but as if her body were absentminded. She was staying at [Dr. Bright's] at the time.* The rain came down and the house leaked. There was some sort of complication. Neither lady wanted to leave the ship. Both felt obligated to stay on account of the other. Well, one day I went out to see Lillian—and this is how I found them. Water was streaming down the walls. The floor was a puddle. Lillian, in a chair in the middle of the room, had rubbers on! Over her head she held an umbrella and with her

* Typescript reads Dr. Flanner's.

free hand she was writing poetry! This, I submit, is the best picture of 1935.

ELLIOT: Have you painted it?

JOHN: I have not.

ELLIOT: Have you painted anything? Have you written?

JOHN: Not a thing. I use my palette for a breadboard. I've leased my typewriter to a spider.

ELLIOT: Why don't you paint that? Paint it and title it "Winter in Taos*"; or, if you're afraid of being sued, title it more generally, thus: "Why Artists Need Relief." Speaking of Taos, how is Taos? It will be a new experience for me. I've never seen a place, or the people of a place, after a deluge.

JOHN: Sorry to have to disappoint you. It's the same place, the same Indians, the same sun, everything is the same.

ELLIOT: And the great struggle that's going on in the world between the old and the new, between the past and the future? Taos must be affected by that.

JOHN: If I understand you, Taos is affected not at all, in my opinion.

ELLIOT: But it must be. All over the world the new economics of abundance is struggling to displace the old economics of scarcity. You are aware of that.

JOHN: Verbally.

ELLIOT: The new politics of cooperation is struggling to displace the old politics of antagonism. The new religion of Man to displace the old religions of idols, the new science of Life to displace the old science of matter. All the vitality of the modern world is engaged in this fight, and to be out of it is to be an exile from life.

JOHN: You've come to the wrong place. We are exiles here and love it.

ELLIOT: You mean you try to make yourself love it. It can't be done until you die. Each man has his quota of uneasy potentialities which give him no peace. The world has never known the perfect exile. But it does know the countless those who ask for something worthwhile to do, who ask that they may *be*. Of these people whom life knows, there are two kinds. One kind works for what it wants. The other kind waits.

JOHN: It is easier to wait than work. I've tried both. To work you've got to have something to do. You've heard of unemployment. To wait, all you need

* *Winter in Taos* is the title of Mabel Dodge Luhan's 1935 memoir.

is time and space, and God gave us lots of both. He favored Taos especially in this respect. And besides, my dear Tom, I've done a bit of musing on that matter you just mentioned—the fight between the old and the new. None other than H. G. Wells started me off. The Communists carried on where he stopped. And what is it all about? Those gentlemen have never really thought of what they're writing about. To show you what I mean. Take the old. The old was here, years and centuries ago. It's still here today. It always will be here. It has a big head start on the new. The new can never catch up. Don't you see? By the very nature of the setup, the established will always outweigh innovations, the conservative will always dominate the radical, habit will always bulk larger than originality, the old men of the world will always be too much for youth. So where's the fight? What's the struggle? What's the sense of it? The new may fight but it can't possibly win. It's like pitting a newborn babe against a giant. If by any chance the new ever does catch up to the old, then by that time the new has itself grown old. So what? A flare at the impossible. Much ado about nothing. It's a drama cooked up by those who haven't yet learned how to take it easy. But they talk about leisure. They, the hectic fellows, the warriors for civilization, the rebels, the revolutionaries, they all talk about the desirability of leisure. Leisure, they say, is to come from all this struggle. Doesn't it sound very much like the war to end war? Fight to get leisure. Go through God knows what revolutions to get what these Mexicans around here already have. A fine ideal for modern civilized people. Work like hell and progress to the position already occupied by backward people. Your landladies are workers. I'm a lazy man!

ELLIOT: I've never heard a better brief for doing nothing. In you, old boy, laziness has found its articulate advocate. Then a drink to the world's lazy men.

JOHN: Sure, I'll drink to that. Only those merit good Scotch who sit on their ass. You say, *be*. I go you one better and say how to be. Be lazy, says John Woodward, ex-artist. Here's mud in your eye. Swell stuff, excellent stuff, a real treat after the rotgut you get around here. It's strange but true—and you'll find it so, a custom of the old Southwest—our best people give you the worst liquor. They cordially invite you to come and be burnt out. That's nothing, however. What I want to say is this: Now that my belly is warm, now that I've declared my creed and gotten myself off my mind, I want to ask how you are. How are you, Tom?

ELLIOT: A year older than when you saw me last.

JOHN: Have a good trip? Oh—forgot—I asked you about that.

ELLIOT: There's one thing I didn't tell you. You know how you feel when Helen seems contrary, when she tolerates what to you is intolerable, when she shows no active interest in what you value, when she seems to not want what you want, in short, when she seems to be going against you—and all your feelings rise up to declare that it's a wife's duty to move with her husband? You know what you do? You make it worse than it is. You protest against everything she does and does not do. Protests, many of them held in, pile up till soon you are protesting against everything, life itself, even yourself. You put up a wall and rail at it. From behind this wall you rave to yourself, "If she doesn't want what I want, I won't want it either."

JOHN: Right you are.

ELLIOT: Unable to change her—and how could you, when you've cut her off—you're determined to punish her. Punishment, curiously enough, takes a form expressed thus, "Neither will I do what I want to do." And you don't. You stop making effort. You get a perverse satisfaction because you know that in defeating yourself you're defeating her, too, since her life is so bound up with yours. In silence you go about accusing her, fuming to yourself, "Look, woman, this is what you've brought about." Occasionally you let off steam in a vehement outburst about something miles removed from the main issue. The rest of the time you drag your tail about the house or stalk from the house as if you were leaving it forever. Other than this, you do less and less until finally you do absolutely nothing. Thus having cut yourself off from your goal, you feel choked. You become bitter.

Then comes a time when a flash of sincere self-criticism makes you ashamed of yourself. To remove this shame you try to justify yourself. To the degree that you succeed in justification, you're confirmed in doing nothing. Time passes. One day you awake to realize that you've been going down, down into a pit of bitter inertia from which it is most difficult to arise. You feel an awful thud and fear that your protests and your punishment have got the better of you. This sudden shock hits some spring in you—and on the rebound, after long disuse, you actually try to do something again. The machine is rusty. You're so out of practice that you feel incompetent and inferior when you try to get into practice again. Such feelings are intolerable, so you fall back and give up the attempt. And now you realize that you're trapped in the hole you've dug for yourself. This is how I felt just before I left New York.

The trip across the continent was a release of a sort. The world came into me and I forgot myself. Something out of the ordinary must have happened, for when we began mounting Raton Pass,* I lifted to it. The man in the pit climbed out. This man became the youth of twenty years ago when the world had a sweet core and a bright rim. As a boy at Coney Island, did you ever take a Trip to the Moon? A flimflam contraption, fascinating to a boy's imagination. Remember the sensations? So I felt as we went up the pass; this time I was an adult and it was a Trip to the Sun. Below were the shadows. All above was the radiance of space. The day was vast and powerful. Behind me I could look down upon what I had left. Before me was a magnet more forceful than I had ever felt in the world before. Poverty in the midst of plenty is the economic condition of most people in the modern world. It then occurred to me that poverty in the midst of plenty has been the spiritual condition of most men and women since the year one—and I at last, a human being, was expanding to consume and reproduce the wealth of the universe. As I reached the top and caught that first marvelous sight of New Mexico spreading out, something in me said, "I must dedicate myself to people, to give them a sense or a new world coming into life." Such states, as you know, are difficult to sustain, but mine persisted until I reached this house. I entered it—and who do you think was here to greet me? None other than Hanna Gow.

JOHN: That, I believe, would be called a flop.

ELLIOT: Just that.

JOHN: What did she have to say?

ELLIOT: Baited me. Wanted to know if I had started the revolution against female Fascism.

JOHN: She did, eh? Better look out for her. She's a wildcat. Rub her right and she purrs. Rub her wrong and she claws. Your back already has a scratch or two. Provoke her more and—

ELLIOT: I can imagine.

JOHN: Well, so here you are, on the fringe of the little village of Taos. What are you going to do with yourself all summer?

* Standing at an elevation of 7,800 feet, Raton Pass allows travelers to pass through the Sangre de Cristo Mountains on the border of Colorado and New Mexico.

ELLIOT: Write a book, as a writer should.

JOHN: Wish you luck. What about? The rising tides of Communism and Fascism?

ELLIOT: Not exactly. I have an understanding that I'm working out. I'm giving a picture of human society in terms of automatic behavior on the one hand and conscious behavior on the other. The thesis, in brief, is the more or less obvious one that what is automatic takes care of itself unless irregularities occur, that what is conscious is not taken care of by the general processes of the world, and that, therefore, those who are conscious—if they would function—must build their own worlds. As you can see, it's not a new idea, but my understanding of it and my development and application of it to the modern situation may help clarify the basic needs and desires of many who now see only chaos and a clash of surface phenomena.

JOHN: More power to you. Will it have a Communistic bent?

ELLIOT: It will include Communism—Communism as the most powerful single present-day force working for a new automatism.

JOHN: Milner will be interested. You know Frank Milner? He went to Russia last year and came back bright red.

ELLIOT: Has he influenced any of the people here?

JOHN: Here? Don't make me laugh. The Anglos are bourgeois to the core. The Mexicans already have the land. Our only potential revolutionaries have private property rights. If you ask my opinion, the system of private property ownership will be in vogue in Taos Valley for many a day. By the way, weren't you looking for land last year?

ELLIOT: We surely were.

JOHN: Going to buy?

ELLIOT: That depends. If it were a matter only of our personal desires, I'd say yes. We want to buy and build. That's precisely why we returned this year.

JOHN: Then why don't you?

ELLIOT: We've got to find the general place and the particular spot. People ruled by practical necessity—their choice is made for them. They pitch tent on the best that comes to hand, even if the best be pretty bad. We, for better or worse, are ruled by ideal necessity. In our hearts is our ideal place. All these years we've been carrying it around, looking for its actual counterpart. This counterpart will not be found in the east, we're pretty sure of that. Connecticut and Pennsylvania are lovely, but tame and constricted compared to New Mexico. Besides, they're already made. We want to make. We want to take the raw materials and shape them to our form. We want the land itself to help us circulate, stimulate our expansion, encourage us to be and live as free human beings upon a free earth. The urge to growth should come from the soil. The urge to develop should come from the sun. Here the soil and the sun are right. So we know we want something in New Mexico. But just where among these millions of acres, is *that* plot which we'll recognize and claim as our own? To live in it and cultivate it, finally to be buried and—

JOHN: Never mind about that. It's got you, too. The Southwest is in your blood. You've got to want some of its land and your own kind of adobe house. You get the fever. You want to do things with adobe. You want to mix the mud with straw, get your hands into it, feel it, work it. You want to mold the mixture into bricks, and lay the bricks, and see walls going up. The material is here, enough to build houses for all the people in the world. It's easy to work, it's fascinating to work, once you start you can't stop. Often the fever gets out of hand and you add room after room to your house until the thing is too large and sprawling for any use. Then you start again and swear that this time you'll hold yourself to a simple little place. It's the strangest thing.

ELLIOT: We looked at a piece of land last year. Quite a site, about ten miles out, off the road to Questa. It's like being on a ship in the middle of the ocean. You feel way out. Indeed you feel that perhaps after all you do live in the universe. All around the valley spreads out and you see the mountains at the far rim. Trees, an irrigation ditch, acres of sagebrush, no house. Only a pigpen. It would seem that it has never been farmed, but you know what they say about the soil here. Water it and it will grow anything. We can't find out who it belongs to.

JOHN: You can't?

ELLIOT: The nearest we've come is to be told that it may be tied up in one of those companies formed by the notorious [Mamby]* before he was murdered.

* Typescript reads Mambey. Arthur Rochford Manby (sometimes locally called Mamby)

JOHN: That's the joke. He wasn't notorious until after he was murdered. Why don't you look up the land records?

ELLIOT: They were burned in one of those mysterious fires.

JOHN: They are damn mysterious fires, and they are happening all the time and nobody yet has a clue. But there may be records in the county clerk's office of the taxes paid this past year.

ELLIOT: But there aren't. That's the trouble. We had a lawyer make inquiries. Even he was stumped.

JOHN: Too many owners turned up when we were getting our little place. At least ten of them, each owning a part of a room, part of an acre. They lived all over the map. It isn't difficult to understand why no one has yet dared to set himself up in the real estate business here. Wish you luck. I'd like to see you and Grace established somewhere near Taos. I still firmly believe this is the greatest earth on Earth. Don't ask me to guarantee the inhabitants.

ELLIOT: Who can? It's they who make every paradise a purgatory.

JOHN: Make it a hell, you mean.

ELLIOT: I mean it's up to you to make it a purgatory. But we'll let that pass. To return for a moment to the matter of locale. I've a few thoughts on that matter—if you'd like to hear them.

JOHN: Let's hear them, though what you say now won't do me much good. I'm committed to Taos. All my eggs are in this basket. My choice has been made.

ELLIOT: One should, I think, view an environment in terms of what it actually is, and in terms of its possibilities—keeping in mind the essential fact that not the place itself but your ability to function in it is the most important thing. Having done this there are three main factors to be considered: first, the physical factor, the obvious physical geography of the place; second, the human factor, the people themselves, the obvious living conditions, the subtle human atmosphere; and, third, the supernatural factor, the

---

was murdered and decapitated in Taos in 1929 after building and then losing a vast land empire. He gained claim to the 61,605-acre Antonio Martínez grant by acquiring small holdings from descendants of Martínez by direct purchase, intimidation, harassment, and the use of agents and shell corporations. His greatest coup came when he induced the county to assess taxes on an enormous swath of the grant that the grant holders (poor Nuevomexicano subsistence farmers without sway in the legal system) could not pay, and then bought the land for back taxes, by which means he acquired 15,400 acres for less than $180.

extraphysical, the extrahuman, the soul of the place. Now to comment on these three in turn. Physical New Mexico is magnificent, unqualified. I say yea to it with all my heart. I say yea to adobe Taos. But as to human Taos, I have certain understandable questions and reservations. You, already as permanent resident, will sympathize with me.

JOHN: Don't rub it in. Already I'm envying you your freedom to come and go. A little more and I'll grind my jaw to hold you as I'm held.

ELLIOT: Then grind—and we'll pass it on to the next factor to be considered. As to the soul of Taos, I'm unsure if it is friendly or hostile to me.

JOHN: Listen to the man. The soul of Taos! Has Taos a soul?

ELLIOT: I'm sure it has.

JOHN: Then you're sure of nonsense. Where does it manifest, this soul? In which bit of gossip? In whose neurosis?

ELLIOT: A pointed question, my dear John. Count one for you. But let's not stop there. Illusion and disillusion give different views of unreality.

JOHN: *Now* what do you mean?

ELLIOT: I mean that the world seen through illusion and the world seen through disillusion are similarly unreal. You are now caught in disillusion as formerly you were caught in illusion. Move on to the third position—the real. You took one step when you dropped illusion. Then you stopped dead. You're arrested in your disillusion as so many people are arrested in rebellion. They revolt and never get beyond revolt. But to come back to you. Illusion believes the impossible; disillusion denies the possible—and the possible is the most important thing in life. It is that that keeps you moving.

JOHN: You've gotten off some good lines but where does the soul come in?

ELLIOT: It is in you already. If you had no soul you'd be content. If you had a soul completely developed you'd be happy. Yours is a germ of a soul just grown enough to make you miserable.*

JOHN: You may be right, but what has all this to do with whether you buy land in Taos?

ELLIOT: You led me astray. Having commented on physical and human Taos,

* Tom Elliot's line is related to Gurdjieff's saying, "Happy is he who has no soul; happy is he who has a soul; terrible is it for him who has a soul germinating in him." It is remarkable to find Toomer quoting Gurdjieff now in the summer of 1935, as Toomer made his definitive break with the teacher in the fall of 1934 and the spring of 1935.

I was going on to say that supernatural Taos does strange things to me. I don't support superstition. I am, as you know, biased toward reason. But just this reason, plus certain experiences, leads me to think that while most superstitions are delusions, some few so-called superstitions are our imperfect recordings of that in life which transcends our five senses and our one used brain. I could easily become superstitious in Taos. The minute I get here I feel—something opens up. Night opens the gap wide. Night in Taos . . . that of me which has always lived, the eternal dark "me" submerged, begins stirring. It brings to me the fears a man might have should he be walking a dark road alone and suddenly the rocks crept from their places and the trees spoke in undertones and the air was thick with sinister animation.

JOHN: You'd better stay away from Taos.

ELLIOT: But here I am. Again I'm here, to live another summer.

JOHN: Does Grace feel as you do?

ELLIOT: Not at all. She's quite at home here. She shares all of my positives, none of my negatives. She was ready to buy last year. I held back. She's ready to buy now. Again I will have to weigh and consider.

JOHN: That's not like you. Five years ago it was you who went ahead. What's the matter?

ELLIOT: I've told you.

JOHN: You haven't given me the real reason yet.

ELLIOT: What have I been talking about all this time?

JOHN: You think too much. You try to be too conscious. You complicate what after all is a simple matter. Keep on this way and in another five years, *your* change of life will come. You'll be worse than the landladies.

ELLIOT: That's a happy picture of the future.

Enter Grace *and the* Landladies. *Men rise.* John *has some special words to say to* Grace, *whom he likes and admires, welcoming her to Taos.*

ELLIOT: (*to* Grace) Get the laundry?

GRACE: I got it, and I bought things for dinner tonight, and I ran into several people on the plaza—

ELLIOT: You do deserve something. (*He pours her a drink. Then, speaking to the* Landladies) Scotch for you?

FIRST LANDLADY: (*pushing past him*) Thank you, but first I must tell you about the keys, so as not to forget them. (*She gets a bunch from the ledge over the fireplace, holds them up and begins telling them off.*) This is for the front door. This is for this door. This is for the back door. This is for the icebox. It's outside on the portal, you know. This is for the garage—

ELLIOT: Keys and more keys. The curse of keys under capitalism.

FIRST LANDLADY: Now where was I?

ELLIOT: Once upon a time a key was a symbol of initiation. See what they have come to in these modern days. Must they really be used out here?

GRACE: Nothing has ever been stolen from me.

FIRST LANDLADY: All the large houses have been robbed.

GRACE: When no one was in them. I won't lock the ice box, I simply won't. If anyone needs food that badly—

ELLIOT: All the large houses you say. We'll be quite safe here.

FIRST LANDLADY: You may be but I ask you to consider the things in the house. Now where was I? Oh yes. This is the key to the *escusado.*

ELLIOT: The *escusado?* What's that?

FIRST LANDLADY: (*embarrassed*) It's . . .

JOHN: The outhouse.

ELLIOT: Oh, the privy. A new word for my New Mexican vocabulary. By all means lock it. So a drink then. (*He pours more glasses. Now at last the* Landladies *allow themselves to be seduced. But only for a minute.*)

FIRST LANDLADY: These chairs are rather nice, don't you think? I bought them in the drugstore in Santa Fe. They're not very strong. If you need to stand on a chair, you'll use the hard kitchen chair, won't you?

ELLIOT: With pleasure.

SECOND LANDLADY: About your bed. You wrote you wanted a double bed. Do you think that one will do?

Elliot *arises, solemnly measures the bed with his eyes, shakes his head.*

ELLIOT: Doubt it. We'll test it tonight and see. It's only three-quarters.

FIRST LANDLADY: Mrs. Metchnikof has a large double mattress and spring which she said she'd be glad to lend.

ELLIOT: That's splendid of her. Can't beds be bought in Taos?

Grace *and the* Landladies *exchange doubtful glances.*

ELLIOT: What about it, John? You have beds in your house haven't you?

JOHN: We made the stands ourselves.

ELLIOT: And the springs and mattresses? Borrowed from Mrs. Metchnikof?

JOHN: Helen got them in Santa Fe.

ELLIOT: Are there no stores in Taos, or won't they sell anything?

FIRST LANDLADY: We've made arrangements with the ditch boss to have a man come once a week to irrigate.

ELLIOT: We have an irrigation ditch?

SECOND LANDLADY: Indeed. We've planted a garden for you.

ELLIOT: Splendid. Vegetable or flower?

FIRST LANDLADY: Radishes, onions, cucumbers. . . . The only thing is you'll have to keep the burros out.

ELLIOT: Excellent. Grace, isn't that fine? At least we won't have to go to Santa Fe for radishes, onions, cucumbers, and burros.

FIRST LANDLADY: Oh, Mr. Elliot, one more little matter. I wonder if you'd mind watering the geraniums every morning and evening for the next few days. We put them in day before yesterday and there hasn't been any rain.

ELLIOT: Happy to. John, will you come up and help me?

FIRST LANDLADY: (*rising*) You will find some plants by the gate of the front fence and others just to the east of the house. Now before we go, are you sure there's nothing else you want?

ELLIOT: Can't think of a thing.

SECOND LANDLADY: (*to* Elliot) Thank you for the drink. It was a treat. It isn't often we get such Scotch in the Southwest.

FIRST LANDLADY: (*moving toward the door, glancing at the ceiling*) Apparently the men have stopped for the day. I don't think they'll need be over this room again. Tomorrow they'll work on the roof of the other room and the kitchen. I'm so sorry—we'll be around to help you clean up. Oh, by the way, I almost forgot. You'll be wanting a girl to help you. I'd be careful of the young girls. They speak English but aren't reliable.

ELLIOT: And I suppose the old women are reliable but don't speak English!

FIRST LANDLADY: Exactly. Whomever you get, would you be good enough to give them special instruction about the floors? Nothing wet should be put on the kitchen wooden floor. It should be swept, not washed. This earthen floor in here should be sprinkled and swept with a native broom each morning. You'll find one in there. Our brooms are too stiff. And once a week it must be gone over with fresh mud and a sheep skin.

ELLIOT: How simple it is to keep house in these native houses.

FIRST LANDLADY: If there's anything else you want to know, please feel free to get in touch with us.

GRACE: We will.

FIRST LANDLADY: Goodnight. We hope you'll find everything and have a good first night.

SECOND LANDLADY: Goodnight.

Exeunt Landladies. Grace, Elliot, and John *make faces, give sighs of relief, go toward the table and settle themselves.*

GRACE: Phew! Now do we dare occupy our own house?

First Landlady *suddenly reappears.*

FIRST LANDLADY: Oh excuse me. I forgot to tell you that the best way to reach us is by dropping a card in the post office. We have no telephone.

ELLIOT: (*under his breath*) Thank God for that.

FIRST LANDLADY: Goodnight again.

ELLIOT: (*rising and going toward the* First Landlady) Allow me.

Exeunt Elliot *and* First Landlady.

GRACE: (*to* John) I suppose Tom wants to be sure they're off.

JOHN: He'd better. By the way, Grace, may I ask you a question? Was Tom in a bad way before you left New York?

GRACE: Not that I know of. What do you mean? He was tired. Nothing else. Why do you ask?

JOHN: Something he said set me wondering.

GRACE: Our last two weeks were quite strenuous. Night after night we had people to the house, all with something to say and eager to say it, all with different and often clashing views of the trouble and remedy of the modern world. Both of us felt the strain.

JOHN: I'm sure you did. There was nothing else?

GRACE: If there had been, Tom would have said so. He always comes out with it. Says that's the only way. Says if you hold something in beyond a certain point, it invariably gets hold of you.

JOHN: Thank you. I suspected one of his psychological tricks—though I shouldn't call this a trick. Oh, I've a message for you from Lillian.

GRACE: How is she? Where is she?

JOHN: She's pretty well, considering. Taos has built her up; the people of Taos have worn her down.

GRACE: What have people done to her? Everybody always loves her.

JOHN: Tried to help her.

GRACE: Then what's the trouble?

JOHN: They've helped her with their right hands and fought each other with their lefts—and all the squabbles have fallen on her head.

GRACE: I don't understand.

JOHN: To give an example. One day I was in Lillian's room. A well-intentioned lady came in bringing fruit. Presently second well-intentioned lady entered bringing wine. Then and there the two good intentions got jealous of each other and the ladies made a scene. That's what Lillian is in all the time.

GRACE: What nonsense. Where is she living now?

JOHN: In a horrible little place off the plaza. Pink walls, no view, an iron bed, one slit of a window, one narrow door. She herself is the only light in the room. Every time I go there I want to take her outdoors and let the sun get into her body.

GRACE: We must get her out of that. We feel responsible. She came out here because of all we said of Taos and the Southwest.

JOHN: Just what is her trouble?

GRACE: Some kind of TB. The doctors discovered it last winter and said she'd have to leave New York. We felt sure this was the place for her.

JOHN: So it is. The place is the best. Her physical tone has improved 100 percent. It's the people who damage her. They are in and out of her room all day. She can't do her work. She can't escape. They see her from the window—and there's no back door. So in general I'd say that hers is a case of looking better and feeling worse.

GRACE: You said you had a message from her?

JOHN: She's going to Santa Fe.

GRACE: Leaving Taos?

JOHN: She said she's had enough of it here. She's been staying on until you and Tom came. She wants to see you at once.

GRACE: We'll go in the first thing tomorrow. I want to see Helen, too. How is she?

JOHN: Coming along pretty well. The child is due sometime this month.

GRACE: I'm very happy for her. She has wanted one so.

JOHN: Yes, she has.

GRACE: Is there a good doctor here?

JOHN: She'll be taken care of. As you can see by looking around, quite a few children have been delivered into the world in New Mexico. No New York specialists—but, somehow or other, the larger part of the human race seems able to get born without them.

Enter Elliot.

ELLIOT: We're going to have a problem with that young lady of ours. She's a sociable young lady, John. If there are children anywhere around, she'll find them. I just found her trying to cross the road to take up with a gang of Mexican kids. There were about ten of them of all ages sitting on a broken wall. The cars come down the highway at fifty and more. She's had no experience with cars. We've got to stop that.

GRACE: (*on her feet*) Where is she?

ELLIOT: In the yard—for how long I don't know. The gate was closed but she found the cattle guard. I'm damned if I see how we're going to keep her in. Nor do we want to. She's got to have children to play with. What's the answer? What about Mexican kids, John?

JOHN: As good as any and better than most. I'll be able to give you firsthand dope in several years.

GRACE: It's getting late. I must fix Betty's supper.

JOHN: And I must go home. I've been away too long as it is.

ELLIOT: And I must get wood for the kitchen stove—and our first dinner in an adobe house on the fringe of the little town of Taos.

Exeunt all.

5

Scene, same as last. The Elliot *bedroom. Nine o'clock the same night. The room is dark. Through the double window comes the luminosity of the Taos night, revealing the dark forms of the room's furniture. Soon the door from the adjoining lighted room opens.* Elliot *enters and quietly closes the door behind him.* Grace, *in the next room, is heard singing a Taos song to put the child to sleep.* Elliot, *keeping the room dark, walks over to the Mexican armchair. As he sits down the leather groans and creaks. Then all is silent for a minute or more.*

ELLIOT: Night in Taos.

Pause.

ELLIOT: When the eyes sleep, the soul comes alive. (*pause*) First the lower soul, the wraith of animals. My animal wakes up, and the march of ghosts is heralded by a dog's bark. No dogs. It is uncommonly quiet. It is silence. The drama of inaction. What forms are sliding down that mountain? In no other region are night and day so different. I wonder if the child will feel it.

Pause. Silence.

Grace *enters and quietly closes the door.*

ELLIOT: Is she asleep?

GRACE: Asleep.

ELLIOT: She stood the trip like a seasoned traveler.

GRACE: She certainly did. No upset of any kind. She was happy tonight. Wasn't cross at all, and she was up late.

ELLIOT: Children adjust quickly.

GRACE: Are we going to have a light?

ELLIOT: Let's not. If we have a light we'll have to draw the curtain. I don't want people peering in from the road. I like to look at that black mountain.

Grace *sits down, lights a cigarette.*

ELLIOT: I suppose we should, though. Have a light, I mean. I ought to give the room a tour of inspection.

GRACE: For what, pray?

ELLIOT: Spiders.

Pause.

ELLIOT: I forgot to ask John if any black widows were around.

GRACE: I've never seen one in Taos.

ELLIOT: But they found them last year. I don't like spiders. I don't like things dropping on me. Any damn thing might fall from that ceiling. And Betty, you know. She calls all crawling things flies. It wouldn't be pleasant if she picked up a fly that happened to be a black widow.

GRACE: Are you worrying?

ELLIOT: No, not worrying. I think we ought to exercise reasonable care. You can get serum from Denver, but it takes several days.

GRACE: How did you find John?

ELLIOT: I actually had a talk with him before you came in. Still has a ton of bricks on his back, but I felt contact with him. Something more than pleasant sitting around. He wants us to buy. How did you find Helen?

GRACE: Much happier. She comes out. I always liked her, but it ended there. We never had anything to say to each other. We have something for each other this time. Lillian is on my mind. Did John tell you?

ELLIOT: Not a thing.

GRACE: We'll talk about her tomorrow. I suddenly feel tired.

ELLIOT: Tired?

GRACE: No, sleepy.

ELLIOT: You might. It's been a long day. Even I feel I might fall asleep at once. It would surprise me, but you never can tell.

In silence they prepare for bed, get into bed.

ELLIOT: Too narrow. Sinks in the middle. Won't do. We'll have to get another bed tomorrow.

GRACE: All right. Goodnight, dear. I hope Betty won't get you up.

ELLIOT: Hope not. Goodnight.

Silence.

A dog barks ferociously as it chases a car down the road. Its bark is answered by barks all over the countryside.

ELLIOT: Now dogs.

GRACE: (*sleepily*) Did you say something?

ELLIOT: I said the dogs.

GRACE: What dogs?

ELLIOT: Didn't you hear them?

GRACE: Must have been asleep.

ELLIOT: You must. They made enough racket to awake the dead. That's a new item in the picture. We didn't have hounds around Alcalde last year.

GRACE: We didn't.

Silence.

Elliot *suddenly sits bolt upright, startling* Grace *from sleep.*

GRACE: What's the matter?

ELLIOT: Give me the flashlight.

Grace *reaches to the side of the bed.* Elliot *grabs the flash and turns it on the pillow.*

GRACE: What's the matter?

ELLIOT: Something dropped from the ceiling. Here it is. Oh, hell. A piece of mud. Another new item. I suppose the damn stuff will fall whenever it feels like it.

Puts the flash out, returns it to the floor by the bed.

GRACE: I'm sorry.

ELLIOT: Isn't your fault. Sorry I startled you. In the morning we'll be awakened by the gods of the roof as they tramp the mud.

GRACE: They'll be over the other rooms.

ELLIOT: And so we won't hear them? This house is like a drum. We'll rattle like a couple of peas. When the gods start pounding I'm going to get up and dance. I mean it. I'm going to dance and sing like hell. I've about concluded that man can assert himself against this country only by singing and dancing. That's why the Indians sing—not love songs but songs to drown out all the other sounds and assert the human will against an overmastering environment. That's why the Indians dance—to have a sense of movement in a country so vast that man otherwise seems stationary. And the Indians are silent—when they are silent—so as to match their stillness against this silence, also so as not to draw attention to themselves when the gods are looking for human prey. Words, in this land, are, on the one hand futile, and, on the other, they are fatal. What chance has a writer against these canyons and mountains, and this night? These, however, are thoughts and perceptions I'll develop at full length in the morning—after I've danced to the beating of the gods of the roof.

Pause.

ELLIOT: Bless me, she's asleep again. Sleep well, my dear. Sweet dreams—and may you not hear the dogs, nor the mud that falls upon thy pillow, nor—what's that?

From a distance, but coming nearer, a group of Indians are heard singing Taos Pueblo songs.

ELLIOT: The Taos Indians—unless I am hearing things. What are they doing around here? I can't be hearing all the way to the pueblo.

He awakens Grace.

GRACE: What is it, Tom?

ELLIOT: Listen.

GRACE: I don't hear anything.

ELLIOT: Listen.

The singing comes nearer, passes by along the road in front of the house, and fades in the distance.

GRACE: Taos boys.

ELLIOT: A bunch of them. They must have been in a truck. Where must they have been?

GRACE: Somewhere toward Cimarron.

ELLIOT: Ten voices, and they filled the night.

GRACE: Shall we sleep now? We've lots to do tomorrow.

ELLIOT: Yes, let's.

They settle themselves under the covers.

Silence.

Curtain.

6

Day in the Southwest. The roof of an adobe house, with a ladder slanting up to it. The Taos Visionary [Ubeam] *is seated in his chair. The* Taos Kid [Buck Fact] *reclines on the roof, his body supported by the raised edges of the corner.*

Ubeam *rises to a stand, facing east, and lifts his right arm in a gesture suggestive of the Nazi salute.*

UBEAM: Hail to thee, rising sun!

BUCK FACT: Sit down. The sun rose three hours ago.

Ubeam *sits down.*

UBEAM: This is a great day, as all the days of Taos are great. Here the soul, shrunken in cities, may expand. Here the lungs of the city streets may breathe freely and become clean. Here the heart has quickened beat, pulsing blood for creation.

BUCK FACT: For once you are right. I don't know a thing about the soul, the heart and the lungs, but it is a great day. It's a pippin, it's a peach, it's a knockout. Nonetheless, I don't see why Taos has to think it is the gem of New Mexico and get high hat. It's not the highest point, by a damned sight. It lacks some 7,000 feet to having the altitude of North Truchas Peak. How would the soul feel on North Truchas, elevation 13,000-odd feet? How would the heart and the lungs fare up there?

UBEAM: In his search for the proper setting of a great culture, man has ever tended to select a majestic spot. Witness Babylon, witness Alexandria, Athens, and Rome. What is New York? A center of commerce, not of culture. Never will it be a center of culture: it is too flat and narrow. Its surroundings are unimposing. By what is it surrounded? Taos is bordered by the greater mountains. New York is bounded by Hoboken and the Bronx. Come to us, ye New Yorkers, we have space for you! Come to us, you of Chicago, Omaha, and San Francisco! Ye of London, come from your fog! Ye of Paris, come from your [plush]*! Here in Taos is the center of the future. Hugh

* Word obscure.

Ferriss[*] will design our city. Frank Lloyd Wright will place houses over the acres. We will have the great engineers, the best doctors, the finest education in the world. And Einstein will come. And amongst us will arise a leader greater than Mussolini, Hitler, Stalin, or Roosevelt!

BUCK FACT: And we'll have distinguished visitors and feel important because of them. This Southwest, it just draws everybody. Nor need we especially invite people from Texas, Oklahoma, and Colorado. Note well that he makes no mention of writers and artists. Are we to suspect that he covets these jobs for himself? Hold on. You speak as if I weren't here already. I, be it known to you, am the world's greatest butcher, a proletarian. Notice me, you puff. For all your words, what can you do? If somebody gave you a cow you'd have to let it rot until hunger drove you to imitate the buzzards. Speak to me, you burro. Bray this way. Stop [hollering][†] for great names. Attend to the life around you, and know that there is more dignity in your Mexican driving his burro up the road than in all the names of men you spout. Let's keep Taos small.

Guess that will hold him.

UBEAM: The morning is bright. One can never tell what afternoon will be. It is the drama and excitement of this land that the weather is unpredictable. This afternoon a storm may come, sloping its dark mass over Taos Mountain, with lightning and thunder and a high wind. Down to the earth the clouds will fall. This is the land of the falling clouds.

BUCK FACT: He said it right that time. Our smallest raindrops are the size of a quarter of a dollar. When they sock you in the eye you know it. Sometimes it hails hail the size of hen eggs. I've seen the tops of cars punctured by as many as sixty holes. Yup, it doesn't bother to rain. The clouds themselves fall right down to earth in streamers. And as for rainbows! Look out, kid, the country will get you and you'll be a poet yet.

UBEAM: I have no words for those who foolishly desire immediate perfection. Let them die and go to heaven. I speak to the men and women who are willing to grapple with conditions. I have no words for those whose eyes

* Hugh Ferriss (1889–1962) was an influential American architect and delineator. His 1929 book, *The Metropolis of Tomorrow*, is a moody, modernist, futurist aesthetic vision for urban planning. Hugh Ferriss, Jean Toomer, Mabel Dodge Luhan, and Tony Lujan all attended the Gurdjieff group of Alfred Richard Orage together in 1925.

† hollowing

are upon the past. Let the past swallow them. I speak to those who live in today for today and tomorrow. America is of and for the future, Taos particularly. This is still raw country. The raw materials are here in great abundance. We have ore. We have soil for crops. This earth is fertile. Even the deserts flower. With water and straw this mud will make a house. Even so, even as we have learned to ditch this earth and make grow things that never grew before, let us learn to water the human soul. There is sun enough. I speak to the builders of a new world.

BUCK FACT: Speak then to the workers. Use words that mean something to a butcher. Stop wasting your words on the artists and intellectuals. They are finished. No more growth is in them. Each of them thinks he knows best and knows it all. Each believes he is the returned Christ. They are egocentric fools. What's the word I just used? Each one is for himself. Not one of them gives a damn for the rest. Let them look to the Indians and learn how to think of the community. I see them in their outlandish garbs strutting around the plaza. They are here in this remote spot of this adobe planet in the hopes of escaping the revolution. They'll get fooled. I hear of their goings-on. Hells bells, the more I see of them the more I'm a Communist—not for myself but for them. It is they who need Communism, not the workers. The workers already know what to do with themselves—and are doing it. Something is needed to give these parasites something to do, teach them how to cooperate, keep them out of mischief and away from each other's throats, prevent them from throwing up houses all over the place. I know what you'll say: you'll say that the building of houses gives us workers employment. The hell you say. Say I, I'm a butcher, but if I were a house-building laborer I'd rather starve.

7

*He stops abruptly, breathless.**

ELLIOT: The altitude seems to get me. So does an empty stomach. Now for

* In this context, it appears that the scene opens with Tom Elliot performing his own rendition of a Pueblo dance. In Toomer's holograph manuscript, the direction to stop abruptly begins a page that is numbered one, suggesting that the beginning of this scene is likely intact. No preceding scene with further description of the dance is extant.

breakfast. Afterward, if I remember aright, I am to develop at length certain ideas with respect to the wisdom of the Indians, the soundness of their psychology and art, their being what they are, this being the tremendous country it is. *(specially to the* Landladies) You, as parties vitally concerned with the future of civilization in the Southwest, are invited to remain and attend.

He makes for the kitchen.

FIRST LANDLADY: *(gazing spellbound after his retreating form)* Well, I never.

GRACE: Tom is certainly in a strange mood.

FIRST LANDLADY: You call it strange? Does New Mexico usually—

GRACE: Not at all. It stimulates him as it does me, but I've never seen him carry on. He is so even tempered that this comes as a great surprise. Perhaps after five years of marriage I'm going to see a man I've never seen before. He didn't sleep well last night.

FIRST LANDLADY: Doesn't seem to have reduced his spirits any.

GRACE: You are right.

SECOND LANDLADY: He was wonderful.

FIRST LANDLADY: *(sitting on her)* You mustn't encourage such antics in men. The Indians' dances are sacred to them. Mr. Elliot will be ashamed of himself. *(Then to* Grace, *as she remembers important matters connected with the house)* I meant to tell you. This door. The door of this room locks on the inside, and you can't open it from the outside. Now the kitchen door, you've got to use a key to open it either way. The door of your child's room has a Yale lock and opens from the inside. I hope you discovered all this and weren't inconvenienced.

GRACE: *(with a wry smile)* I discovered it. Tom locked up last night and put the keys in his pocket. As I didn't want to disturb him this morning, and as Betty was sleeping when I got up, I found myself locked in the kitchen.

FIRST LANDLADY: I'm so sorry.

GRACE: I was mad. I don't usually get mad over trifles.

FIRST LANDLADY: When you want a bath, there's a rubber tub left by the last tenant. It's in this closet, I believe. *(She goes to the closet and pokes in.)* Yes, there it is. I won't bother to bring it out. Now about the garbage. If you ask him, the man across the way will be glad to have it for his chickens. Just put it out in front of the kitchen door, and he'll call for it every morning. Now let me see, what else? When you need to dispose of your cans, you know where the dump is.

GRACE: Who can miss it? Right on the highway. Couldn't civic pride find a more concealed spot? Or is Taos proud of its consumption of canned goods? I once went to a dance where the Indians symbolized the presence of the white man by a heap of tin cans.

FIRST LANDLADY: The Indians themselves use canned foods.

GRACE: Of course, now that we have taken nature's supply from them. The land stealers and the poachers play right into the hands of our large canned-food concerns. But you won't find the dump heap in their front yards.

FIRST LANDLADY: They throw them where they use them. The tires of my car have been cut. Every time I go into a pueblo I get a puncture.

GRACE: If I were them I'd strew the roads with tacks and nails. You know what they say when you talk with them. If he is a friend of yours, the Indian will begin—"Tourists today." You ask, "Many?" He says, "Many." You ask, "This morning?" He says, "Early this morning." You ask, "This afternoon too?" He says, "This afternoon too. All day, many tourists come." He doesn't seem to mind. Of course he does, but he won't let you see it. They are too patient, too tolerant.

FIRST LANDLADY: They are fatalists. They haven't the white man's will.

GRACE: Nor his curiosity.* Imagine having strange people descend on you at all hours of the day and poke about.

FIRST LANDLADY: There are worse things in life.

GRACE: By the way, we'll need ice at once. Who is the iceman, and how does one find him?

FIRST LANDLADY: When we leave here we will go right by his place. I'll be glad to leave word.

GRACE: Thank you. That will be a help. I've a hundred things to do this morning and I suppose I had better get started right away. The electric company. Groceries. Milk. I made a long list while I was locked in the kitchen.

FIRST LANDLADY: We must be going, too.

* Line editing in Toomer's hand removes the word callous from "callous curiosity."

Elliot *reappears.*

ELLIOT: Where's Betty? Don't see her anywhere.

GRACE: She managed to get out, even if you did hide the keys.

ELLIOT: Hide them? Were you locked in?

GRACE: *(a trace of anger returning)* Of course I was.

ELLIOT: Sorry. *(gets the bunch from his coat pocket)* Here you are.

GRACE: You might unlock this door while you're about it.

Elliot *does so, a bit sheepishly.*

ELLIOT: What about Betty?

GRACE: Twice she started across the road. Twice I stopped her. Then I thought I had her playing by herself in the yard. Then next thing I know she had crossed the bridge behind the house over there and there she was, making friends with a dozen kids on the other side of the creek.

ELLIOT: Fast work. As was to be expected. What kind of kids?

FIRST LANDLADY: There's a group of houses over there, a small village. I know two of the families. They are nice people. Your child will be all right with them.

ELLIOT: Cars?

FIRST LANDLADY: Few. They have to go slow when they cross the stream.

ELLIOT: That's good.

GRACE: I'm going to town. Want to come?

ELLIOT: Should I?

GRACE: There's much to do, but don't unless you want to. I can manage.

ELLIOT: Can you? Believe I'll stay here. I have a feeling that if I don't get to work this morning I never will. Must plunge in at once, that kind of a feeling. I'll go down with you this afternoon.

GRACE: All right. The car keys?

Elliot *produces them.*

GRACE: The key to the garage?

Elliot *produces it.*

Grace *gathers some things from the table and starts off, the* Landladies *following.*

ELLIOT: Betty?

GRACE: Shall I take her?

ELLIOT: Wish you would. I'd like about an hour of solid work. Will you stop in and see Lillian? Might ask her and whoever else you want to come out at five o'clock for the deserving hour.

Grace *nods and goes out. Then the* Landladies *nod goodbye and follow her.*

Elliot *has combed his hair. Otherwise he is as he was when dancing, a pair of trousers over pajamas. Without bothering to change, he sets his typewriter on the table, opens it. Gets paper. Pulls out his briefcase. Lays hold of his manuscript, sits down in the Mexican chair, and tries to get into his work. His difficulties begin. The words he has written mean nothing to him. The world of his book is a remote world, the door locked, the key lost. He frowns and strains, shifts position. Smokes. Tries to concentrate and move himself into the spirit of his writing. As a last resort he puts paper in the machine and types away, putting down anything that comes into his head. On reading what he has written he gives a snort of disgust, rips the paper from the machine, crumples it, and hurls it at the wall. After cursing, he slumps in his chair, stares ahead, dogged and determined though beaten.*

ELLIOT: What in hell's the matter? Haven't written a word in a month. Should be fresh. Should be full of things. To whom am I writing? For what? There's an answer, but I don't feel it. To whom is it important that I write what I think about man—automatic man, conscious man, automatic society, conscious society? To whom? Not for myself. I know what I think. Not for Grace. I talk it to her. Not for my landladies. What would it mean to them? Not for my friends, they're tired of thinking—and, besides, the only subject that interests them is economics or politics. What's the answer? I'm damned if I'll write to these walls. These walls . . . this roof. (*he looks up, now he hears the men still tamping on the roof*) There's a story, the epic of the roof. I could write a story all right, if I were a story writer. Useless philosopher that I am. Well, then, a letter. That's it. A letter to old Bob. Must write something to justify my staying home.

He puts fresh paper in the machine and begins pounding. Soon there is a knock on the door. He goes to the door of his room, opens it, and sees nobody. He goes to the window, looks out, and sees a man at the kitchen door.

ELLIOT: (*calling*) Come around here. There are three doors to this house and I'm at this one.

He goes back to the door and waits.

ELLIOT: Good morning. What can I do for you?

MAN: I have wood. You need wood?

ELLIOT: Yes. How much? What kind?

MAN: Piñon. Good wood. Dry. Two burros. One dollar.

ELLIOT: Two burro loads? I thought that was a vanishing industry. Glad to know it is still alive. Sure, I'll support it. I'll take both loads.

MAN: Where you want it?

ELLIOT: Heave it over the fence. Doesn't make any difference where, just so long as it's on this side here. Wait. Take the dollar now and you won't have to bother me again.

He closes the door and goes back to his typing. After a time he interrupts himself, thinking it best that he go out and see if the wood is really there. He returns carrying two pieces of piñon, holding one to his nose.

ELLIOT: The old bandit didn't jip me. That odor! Nothing else like it. The odor of the Southwest. Whenever I smell it, I see New Mexico. Wish I could light a fire. Maybe tonight. But you should smell the smoke. Guess I'll have to light my own fire, get on my own roof, and smell my own smoke. Not enough houses nearby. That's the thing you get in Santa Fe. Remember, my boy, how a haze of piñon smoke arises from the old city every evening around five o'clock? I'll miss that up here. This place is too open and windblown.

With some ceremony, he places the pieces of wood on his table, one on each side of the typewriter.

ELLIOT: I must make a ritual of it. Piñon deserves religious sentiments, a chant invoking the aroma, a dance invoking the smoke. Now! Shelley—or was it Keats?—who had his rotten apples.* I have my piñon. Now for a masterpiece, if only a letter.

Again he pounds the machine.

After a time a sight in the yard catches his eye. He jumps to his feet.

ELLIOT: Damnation. How'd they get in? Thought this place had a cattle guard. An old bony nag and a cursed donkey. Better let them know who's master here.

[Goes out,]† and is heard chasing them, shouting, "Scaboose! Vammoose! Get the hell out of here! Scaboose, you nag! Vammoose, you ass!"

He returns, wiping his hands as if he'd had a man-to-man hand-to-hand tussle with the beasts.

ELLIOT: Not exactly a neighborly act—but, not in vain shall my landladies have planted radishes.

He smells one piece of piñon, then the other, his face taking on a beatific beam. Again he sits down and pounds the machine.

Presently there is another knock on the door.

ELLIOT: *(without stopping typing)* Here I am, in here. Enter, be you devil or angel.

When no one appears he jerks to his feet, and shouts—

ELLIOT: There are three doors to this house, and I'm at this one.

* Elliot alludes to Friedrich Schiller, the German Romantic poet and playwright (1759–1805) who famously kept rotten apples in a desk drawer to allow their scent to inspire his creativity. English writer George Eliot (1819–1880) was fascinated by Schiller and reported that the apples reminded Schiller of his mortality.

† Out goes out.

He goes to the door, opens it, and waits.

ELLIOT: Around here. Yes?

MAN: I'm the iceman.

ELLIOT: What? How'd you guess?

MAN: Miss Murphy phoned Mat Gross and he got me at the gas station as I was passing.

ELLIOT: This morning?

MAN: Just now. I was coming thisaway so I came right out.

ELLIOT: And I thought this was the land of *mañana*. I was mistaken, I see. Yes, we need ice. The box is on the portal. It is the one thing I didn't lock up last night. Fill her up. Keep her filled. Send in your bill whenever you're hard pressed.

MAN: We have tickets. They are punched each time. Cost you five dollars.

ELLIOT: Very well. Here's the five. Don't forget the ice. I know I shouldn't, but the minute you get businesslike I get suspicious.

He closes the door and returns to the typewriter.

Grace *enters, several packages in her arms. She puts them down.*

ELLIOT: Hello. Back so soon? Get everything done?

GRACE: All for this morning. The minute I let Betty out of the car she made a beeline for the children over the bridge.

Grace *and* Elliot *regard each other in silence.*

GRACE: If I had tried to stop her, she'd have cried. It would have ended by my putting her in her room.

ELLIOT: What's to be done? What *can* we do?

GRACE: She's always been a social child, and we've been glad, but I've never seen her like this. It's a craze. She's crazy to be with those children. I had a hard time to get her to leave them to go with me to town. On the way, I asked her what she did over there. She said she played with the [children]* and saw horses and cows. You know how she loves animals. They seem to have everything back there—goats and sheep and pigs. I can easily see, we won't see much of her.

ELLIOT: But she's too young to be let go off by herself all day.

GRACE: Of course she is. That's what's worrying me.

ELLIOT: Words can't be used to control her yet. We can't be sure she understands. Nor can she control herself. Her legs are better than her judgment. She'll eat anything. We don't know who is back there. There may be sick people, for all we know. Don't like the setup.

GRACE: Neither do I. When I was at Lillian's the county nurse came in.

ELLIOT: You saw Lillian?

GRACE: *(nodding)* I told the nurse we have a problem with our child and Mexican children.

ELLIOT: What did she say?

GRACE: I asked her what to do. She advised giving her shots for typhoid and smallpox, and letting her go ahead.

ELLIOT: Hmm. Like a good member of the profession, she thinks only of the physical side.

A pause, weighted. Grace, *who has been standing all the while, now takes a chair on the other side of the table and lights a cigarette.*

ELLIOT: How's Lillian?

GRACE: Better than when she left New York, but not well. She's in a horrid little place. We must find something better for her. If only she had a car. Horrid pink walls, only one window and that on the court. She can't see a thing. What's the use of being here unless you feel you are in the country and see the mountains and the sunsets? It's frightfully dusty in town. All the roads cut up. Lillian gets that part of it, all right. She's only a block from the plaza. She's been in Taos a month. This is the third place she's had—and it's worse than the others. How can people build such coops in a country like this?

* childrens

ELLIOT: Coops in the universe. Small houses in a vast land. Small people in vast spaces. Perhaps they feel secure only when they are jammed together. All of which is an extra argument—if we needed one—pointing to the necessity for a place of our own. We ought to have a place—and guest houses for friends of ours like Lillian. What can we do here, in this house? Our hands are tied. We've hardly room enough for ourselves.

GRACE: The kitchen is cramped.

ELLIOT: I wouldn't call this room large.

GRACE: We must talk to her this afternoon. She's coming for tea. Bill Bryne is driving her out.

ELLIOT: Who's Bill Bryne?

GRACE: He came in while I was there. A tall young fellow who seems devoted to her. You'll like him. Intelligent, good feelings. Seems to have been about a lot. He talked about Mexico. Lillian wants to go there, you know.

ELLIOT: I didn't know. To Mexico? In her condition? I wouldn't go there myself at this time of year.

GRACE: You know Lillian. She goes where she wants—and gets there. Frank Milner dropped in, too.

ELLIOT: What is he like? John was talking about him. Been to Russia. Did he talk Communism?

GRACE: No, he didn't. He was very quiet, in fact. A solid sincere kind of person. He too seems devoted to Lillian. I've seen it happen again and again, but it never ceases to amaze me, the way people become devoted to her. I know what it is, because I feel it. It began the first time I saw her, eighteen years ago.

ELLIOT: The same with me. She evokes strangely pure impulses in people. You want to help her—but it isn't all that. In fact, it's the other way around. People go to her for help. Half the time I don't believe they are conscious of what they are getting. There's a purity and singleness in her that helps them integrate themselves. I've never heard her advise anyone—yet they get direction. To see such courage in so frail a body, such an uncompromising spirit when so many things have broken against her. Really, there's a religious essence in Lillian. Her best poems are pure prayers. She's a priestess of some kind, and in New York she lives on Broadway, and in Taos she lives just off the plaza. Now I see what will happen, and why. Taos, like New York, will lose her. She'll have to leave, in order to protect herself. She won't be able to be herself and to maintain herself for too long. Wherever she is, an excess of people drive her away. She can't and she doesn't want to lock herself in. That's the cell idea, the monastery, the nunnery. It isn't living. But neither can she digest and transform more than [her]* quota of poison. The people of our civilization don't yet know how to use such a person. We are like children. All of our acts are unconscious—hence egocentric, hence unreliable. As long as we are moved by good impulses we are fine. We feed her, as she feeds us. But, as a child does, we often thoughtlessly overdo—and we can't check ourselves. We'll give her more than she can handle. We'll turn on each other and begin fighting with each other as to who is to give most, who is to get most—and all of it will fall on her. She has no means of protecting herself from what she can't handle. There she sits in her room. She has to take all, the good, the bad, and the indifferent. Her body can't stand up. As children wear adults out, so Taos will drain Lillian. That's why she's thinking of Mexico already. You see what I mean? It isn't only that we are children. It is also that the spiritual dimension of our lives is without body like Lillian's. It is exposed, unorganized, and vulnerable. It is by itself, each spark alone, unprotected by rituals and ceremonies. There is no tradition, no custom to establish the relationships between people and a person like Lillian. She, individually, has to do it all herself. Not that the relationship should fit into rigid patterns. Not at all. But there should be some form, some simple rules taking care of such simple matters as when she may be seen, for how long, by how many. Even a doctor has his office hours. Lillian does not want a church, that would be the end. But she should at least have a secretary, someone to tell people when it is time to go.

GRACE: Have you been writing?

ELLIOT: Yes, but not seriously. I mean not on the book. Couldn't get into it. A letter to Bob. Began it the other night in Pueblo.† Like to hear it?

GRACE: Of course.

Elliot *gathers his pages and reads.*

* she

† Pueblo, Colorado.

Dear Bob,

To motor across the continent is to let the physical world into you. In comes the world of earth—and out go your thoughts and feelings and even your ego. You sit in your car, you pass through the changing landscapes of the states, and you become a mirror. Increasingly you become what you see—the fields, the hills, the unending road before you; decreasingly you cease to be what you are. I am New Jersey, Pennsylvania, Ohio, Indiana, Illinois, Iowa, Nebraska, Colorado, New Mexico. . . . I am not Tom Elliot, which is a good thing, perhaps.

Though you, like myself, are a man of extremes, you probably would not experience the extreme of this, simply because you do not live most of the year in New York. To live in New York where man has banished nature almost entirely, and then suddenly to make a trip such as the one we've just had. . . . From a house in the metropolis to a car on the open road, from the problems of life to the simple problems of a car, from books to maps, from the typewriter to the steering wheel, from strenuous discussions to questions of roads, from late hours to early to bed and early to rise . . . it is great, but, as I say, it is also an extreme change, and you undergo an extreme change without being aware of exactly what is happening.

Grace and I looked forward to the trip this year, just the trip, even though it would be complicated by Betty's presence. What a year we had! People speak of revolution. I went through two major ones—spiritual, however. Twice I died. Twice, somehow, I was born again. Tired when the season began, these revolutions tapped fresh energies while they were in progress but I was flatter than ever in the aftermath—nor had I for myself a five-year plan. In addition, I let the world of economics collide with me. As you know, for several years I have steered clear of economic issues, feeling that I knew nothing about them and they were not for me. One by one my New York friends became involved. I stood off. My reasons were sound. My values were excellent. But what did I find? I found myself not only out of the current but out of life. Soon it became apparent to me that the only live issues were those in which economics and politics were involved. People came to the house. In the past we had had meaning for each other. Now our meetings were quite meaningless. Soon after dinner they went dead. They remained dead until Communism or Fascism or social credit* or some economic

* Social Credit was an economic and political movement inspired by the ideas of C. H. Douglas. Social creditors differed from traditional economists in that they saw purchasing power, not goods, as scarce. (Tom shows the influence of this idea when he speaks of a "new economics of abundance . . . struggling to displace the old economics of scarcity.") They believed that wartime measures of price control and planned economy should be continued in peacetime and that providing the unemployed and working classes with dividends from excess production could create a healthy economy and raise the standard of living for all instead of just the wealthy classes.

plan or other was broached. At once they were revived. This was a phenomenon which I might deplore but not ignore. So I faced it, to find its meaning, to establish my relation to it. Where did I stand? It was more than intellectual curiosity; my functioning, namely, my life itself was at stake. What could I contribute to a world whose predominant interests were those of economics and politics, I being neither an economist or a politician? In attempting to answer these questions I had, of course, to open myself to the current proposals and their respective camps—not only to the ideas and personalities but also to the powerful suggestions that are in the air, emanating from these camps. I opened wide, reserving one right only, namely, the right and the duty that I maintain my integrity and balance. And thus another large meal was taken into my system, taxing my powers of digestion and assimilation—just the powers that have been most severely taxed, if not overtaxed, during the past decade. I was flooded. I was deluged. I was offered more than I could possibly digest and understand—unless I were willing to devote the rest of my life to an understanding of economics and politics.

Nothing happens gradually anymore. Leisurely adjustments are of the past. No time is allowed for transitions. Not much time is allotted for the regular processes. It does seem that in this respect the philosophy of the Communists is accurate, namely, it does seem that revolution is a form of evolution, and that we live in a revolutionary era. Reflection and contemplation are shelved. You are supposed to hear an idea—and not think about it but act. And I, who believe that you should understand before you act, am outmoded. Education is suspended. Propaganda holds sway. And I, who in my time have at least fancied myself a teacher of men, found myself in the position of being a target for propaganda the aim of which was—I will not say conscript—but to enlist my actions along lines laid down by others.

Communists came to the house. They were sincere men who believed they held the only key to the future. They were vital. They were alive with the release of energy which occurs when numbers of people join together in a movement whose action ideas are dramatic and simple, whose aim is to serve mankind. They had a sense of purpose, a sense of adventure. They were courageous. They had guts. They were tense if not intense, as men are when they are constantly up against difficulties and dangers. They were strenuous, as propagandists usually are. They were selfless, in so far as they had surrendered themselves and their lives to the cause of Communism. They were egotistical, in so far as they felt themselves, as a community, superior to you, a bourgeoise intellectual. They were ruthless, as men are who believe that the end justifies the means. They were cruel, as most people are when they are severely pressed by circumstances. All of them had the strength of a limited view. All of them were under the delusion that Communism is a complete idea, a body of ideas which will serve man in all of his aspects. Most of them were dogmatic, uncritical of their own views, most critical (dogmatically) of other people's views. All of them were under the powerful suggestion that Communism is the thing. You can imagine me in the midst of such men, none of whom were at a loss for words or for the energy with which to project their words, hour after hour, night after night—and each night late. First they began to instruct me, as if I were a dunce with possibilities, as if I knew absolutely nothing of social conditions and economic ideas, that is Communistic economic ideas, but had the capacity to learn quickly, by great gulps, and then act along their lines. I swayed between interest, admiration of their energy, enthusiasm, and intensity, amusement at their naive assumptions, protest against their egotism, sympathy and agreement with certain of their values. Soon I awoke to the fact that I was always on the defensive because I had no counterproposal of equal or greater cogency and practicality. I got mad, not mad at them but mad at myself, mad at the world situation which threw me into such a situation. Then I turned about and became active, expressing my views and making them meet me. All went better after that.

Fascists came to the house—at any rate they said they were Fascists. They were less interesting, less stimulating than the Communists. They were not in action yet, because, so they said, the Communists were not as yet a challenge much less a menace. They pooh-poohed Communism and Communists, saying that the Communist party was a joke, that Communists were not and never would be a power in this country.

One monarchist came. His views interested me very much.

Social creditors came. They were intelligent people with good feelings—my kind of people on the whole but they lacked dynamics. Babes in the political woods, not a chance have they against the old-time politicians on the one hand or the Jesuitical Communists on the other. Though unable in so short a time to understand Communism or capitalism, finance or social credit, I did manage to clarify many things for myself. More than ever I was convinced that economic and political struggles were not for me, that my function was elsewhere. In brief, I formulated my position thus. That I was in no position to judge which of the proposals were best suited to bring about the obviously needed changes of social conditions; that I would favor whichever actually did the job; that I myself was already ready for a new order of society; that I, without any more revolution, was already ready to inhabit a future world. So far, so good.

I soon realized, however, that a definition of my position did not solve the question of my function. My position, thus defined above the battle, left me high and dry. As long as I maintained it I could do no more than wait, wait for the world to catch up with me—but waiting can hardly be called a function; I realized, in fine, that it was as sterile to be too far in the future as to be too far in the past. I was a living man. My life placed me in contact with the immediate scene and its issues and struggles. I already *was*, I had and was my own being, timeless; but in order *to function* I had to have a vital and useful relationship to the struggling world of men. Someone quoted Romain Rolland* to me to the effect that even though you were at the gates of heaven it was your duty to return to [the] world and participate in the struggle for the literature of the world's people.† I pondered that quotation, as it aroused quite a response in me. I pondered many other matters of a similar meaning.

Meanwhile, I gave myself and was given no rest. The momentum started by my initial plunge gained way. Indeed it increased far beyond my expectations. I was swamped. I was overwhelmed. There were lunch dates. People came in around five o'clock. Every single evening was filled. Each full evening drew forth discussions. The last two weeks was a whirlwind. And then we left.

How we wanted to leave! After all that Communism and capitalism, economics and politics, to regain our balance by experiencing parts of the country, and the people therein, remote from New York and its untypical obsessions, I mean untypical of the rest of America. To catch our breath. To rest. To let the body live in physical surroundings, the mind and the emotions asleep or drowsing.

One day we were in the thick of it in New York. The next, without gradation or transition, we were in our new Ford, the top down, only ourselves and the baby, rolling through neutral New Jersey, then lovely Pennsylvania. I should note, however, that New Jersey was not altogether neutral this time. There was a strange haze in the air. It reminded me of the haze seen around the mountains of the Southwest where there has been a dust storm somewhere. Dirt got in your mouth. Strange sand particles, unlike any others I had ever seen, got onto the seats of the car. I suspected—and my guess was confirmed later—that we in New Jersey were getting the tail end of one of the dust storms that had ravaged Kansas and other states down there. And this was our first taste and sign of the tempests in nature that everywhere over the planet are paralleling the tempests in man.

As I wrote you when there, we stayed over with friends in the Middle West for several weeks, thus breaking the trip. Then off again.

Through Illinois nothing special happened. I never expect it to. To me, Illinois—Chicago excepted—is neutral like New Jersey. All through Iowa we had rain. Sometimes heavy rain, with thunder and lightning. But rain, rain continually. At the hotel in

* French writer Romain Rolland (1866–1944) reports some of the deathbed words of his friend and mentor, the German writer Malwida von Meysenbug (1816–1903): "I have fulfilled my destiny, I can depart. Tonight the gates of heaven will be opened for me; you will accompany me to the threshold; but you must return to earth; you still have many struggles before you. Without struggles we cannot live, without struggles and love" (Rolland, *Letters of Romain Rolland and Malwida von Meysenbug*, 34).

† Toomer struck the adjective "oppressed" before "people."

Council Bluffs they told us they had never seen anything like it. Last year, a drought. This year, rain every day and all day and all night for two solid weeks (and we thought of the deluge they had in Taos, and wondered in what condition we would find our house). In that same hotel I chanced to see the headlines of a paper a man was reading. The headlines ran, "Floods Sweep Nebraska." I became alert at once. This was something I ought to know about, as we would cross—or try to cross—Nebraska the next day. Moreover, just as I never expect anything to happen in New Jersey or Illinois, I always expect something to happen in Nebraska. Every time I've crossed it I've run into extremes of temperature, at least one cloudburst, terrifying clouds, and I'm continually scanning the horizon for a tornado.

I bought a paper. Back in Chicago we had read of the western floods. They had seemed as remote as the earthquake at the base of the Himalayas. This was different. The paper mentioned the Republican River as the worst offender, mentioning the property damage and the loss of life. It was still running high and wild. Now it was just this Republican River that we'd have to cross, if we held to our plan of cutting southward down across Nebraska. The paper mentioned a town at which we had once stopped for lunch. This town, it said, was a total wreck. Grace and I looked at each other, both of us feeling that the uncontrollable forces of nature were, if not hitting us, at least cutting across our path. Had I been superstitious I certainly would have taken it as a sign that God was barring our way and warning us to turn back while there was still time. In fine, I took this flood personally—and there was and still is enough superstition to me to feel a certain menace in it. Then and there we recast our route, deciding to keep to the Lincoln Highway straight across the state, curving south only when we reached Colorado.*

The next morning, not knowing what we might meet, we got an early start, drove through a downpour between Council Bluffs and Omaha, resigned and braced ourselves to another day of storms. However, we had not gone far into Nebraska when to our amazement, the sky began breaking and we saw clear skies to the west. Shortly after lunch we were tempted. Neither Grace nor I had ever seen a flood. Pictures and descriptions of them, yes. But not an actual flood with our own eyes. The risk did not seem great, even with Betty aboard. It was a bright day now, warm and dry. We'd turn south, not with the intention of crossing the river, but simply to see what had happened and return to the northern route. If we saw the water rushing our way, we'd turn around and fly. We went south on a road without number, eyes peeled for the first sign of

* The Republican River Flood of 1935 was the worst flood in Nebraska history. A 350-mile stretch of the Republican River overflowed its width by between three-quarters and one and one-half miles, claiming more than one hundred human lives and killing tens of thousands of livestock while damaging nearly 275,000 acres of farmland (Diffendal et al.).

rampant water. On and on we went. Not a sign of water, not a sign of catastrophe. All the lands and farms we passed were indeed so usual-seeming and peaceful that after a time we became unvigilant. Thus we failed to note the beginning, or, rather, the end of washes on both sides of the road. Suddenly we were pulled up. I jammed on the brake just in time. Ten feet in front of us a bridge had been washed out. Not a post or beam or plank of it was left. Now the creek or whatever it was had toned down, it held to its course, but the muddy water ran swiftly. All around us were signs of the overflow. It was not a large creek, it may have been a small tributary or branch of the river, but what it had done was enough to inform and impress us as to the havoc wrought by the river itself. Over everything was mud. Now mud has always seemed to me to be a harmless, even a pleasant, thing. I recall the mud pies I made when a boy. This mud was repellant, almost gruesome. It was not only that it was out of place, smeared over the grass and weeds. It was that in the very way it was laid down it conveyed the means by which it had been deposited, suggesting upheaval and destruction. There it lay quietly, drying out, earth of the earth, mud of mud. Yet this inert drying stuff sent a shiver through me. As a bird looks at a snake, so I looked at it, a menace that fascinated me. That it was largely idea was demonstrated by Betty who insisted on getting from the car and sporting in it.

On the other side of what had been the bridge, the road was demolished. In some places it had been washed away completely. In others there were miniature canyons and ravines. And then, further above, we caught a glimpse of what may have been a town on the main river. Stuff was thrown about everywhere. Mud was over everything, and I swore that it even coated the leaves of the trees. The one house we saw—what remained—was crumpled over as if one of its sides had caved in, the water pushing the roof on a slant to the ground. Not a soul was in sight. Nothing stirred. The air was filled with the sound of the creek rushing by at our feet, and what may have been the booming of the main river, a rushing swirling sound, angry, like a deep-toned battle drum, like distant thunder.

As I looked and listened there suddenly came into my mind these words: the revolt of nature. The revolt of nature against man. After [ages] of mistreatment at our hands, nature, I told myself, was finally taking her revenge, toppling our structures, washing our works from off her. I, standing there on that last road, seemed like the last survivor, the last human creature permitted to survive in order to witness and record it all, the end of man, and then myself to die, taking the record of an eye witness to Him who was our father and creator.

In New York you get the restlessness, the upheaval and devastation of human society. Out here, you get the restlessness, the upheaval and devastation of the very planet itself. Within my time, in my own experience, both man's and nature's disquiet have increased, the increasing chaos of human life being paralleled by an increasing instability and violence of natural elements and forces. Is there a [causal]* connection between the two? I wouldn't be surprised. At first sight it is maybe difficult to see how the condition of small man could affect the condition of the great earth. Yet small things like germs irritate and infect us. It is quite probable that we irritate and infect the planet. In any case I play with the idea, though it is too serious an idea to be played with. Just how serious it is was brought home to me as I witnessed the havoc wrought by the Nebraska river.

Later we tried to locate the exact spot on the map, without definite success. The map showed no town near where we thought we had been. The house and wreckage we saw may have been washed down to that place by the river. It seems likely but we are not even sure that it was the Republican River. Even as I write about it, it gives me a strange sensation to remember that sense of devastation so vividly yet be unable to place and name it. That lost road, that gruesome mud, that wreckage and the death it meant, that windless stand under the trees, that booming sound—the experience sort of floats in me, in my world yet out of it, a fruitful, haunting event which I cannot pin down. Back on the Lincoln Highway again, we pushed westward in silence. It was a long time before we spoke to each other. Glad to have returned to the world of everyday events, feeling secure in the car and reassured by its swift motion, we nevertheless could not forget what we had seen and felt, and we wanted to get away from it, to have the car speed us away to new places.

Around five o'clock, our gas ran low and we knew we had to stop at the next town. This next town happened to be a town by the name of Ogallala. As we entered the main street we saw people standing around in groups but thought nothing of it. I noticed muddy water flowing in the gutters, but thought nothing of it, either. We were, I was sure, on high ground. Nothing had been said or written about the North Platte River acting up.

At the gas station was all commotion. Men were rushing about, boarding up the doors, throwing bags of sand around the base of the building. One fellow dashed over to give us service, and we managed to get from him the information that the Platte River had broken the dam just above the town, [water]† was rushing in, and they feared that Ogallala, too, like the town south, would be flooded.

Even as our tank was filled, the rush of muddy water increased, swirling into the main street from a side street. In front of us, directly across our road out, we saw a large pool forming. As quickly as we could we got underway. They warned us against

* casual
† watering

the pool. Several cars had already been stuck, they said. We made it, all right, but the water came higher than the running boards. Another half hour, and it would have been impossible to get through.

Now central as well as southern Nebraska was threatened with floods. All of Colorado had been flooded, so the man at the gas station had said. A series of frightful cloud bursts on the eastern side of the Rockies had caused it all. We might not be able to reach Denver. Our one chance, we were told, was to continue due west and north to Cheyenne, Wyoming. Perhaps from there we might get down. As we drove out of Ogallala I had visions of a long detour, reaching New Mexico by the roundabout way of the states to the west of Colorado.

At Cheyenne the next morning we were happy to learn that the direct road to Denver was open, had in fact been opened just that morning. We would strike several bad places which they had not yet been able to repair, a few washouts, a few detours—but we'd get through. So we did.

Between Denver and Colorado Springs, however, the road had completely gone. They sent us on an eighty-mile detour through the mountains. We came out at the base of Pike's Peak. As for Colorado Springs itself, you never saw such a sight. Here, along the river, we witnessed in detail the havoc and wreckage only glimpsed at that spot in Nebraska. Houses were askew, crumpled, some quite washed down. A circus was demolished. Wreckage was everywhere. And mud, unbelievably thick mud, was in and over everything. And this mud too seemed vulgar and gruesome. And again I thought: In New York you get the restlessness, the upheaval and devastation of human society. Out here you get the restlessness, the upheaval and devastation of the very planet itself.

Our trips west, in years past, were comparatively uneventful and peaceful. This year we were fated to run into it, experiencing catastrophe as observers. Next year. . . .

Out of the Springs was another bad place in the road—and then our way was free and clear.

Wakenburg, Pueblo, Trinidad—and then Raton. As we mounted to Raton Pass I felt we were climbing above the restlessness of man and the restlessness of the planet. Devastation slipped off and away and fell back. Catastrophe was ended. No upheaval was here. There never had been and there never could be. This great solid mound of high earth was superior to such things. And as we reached the summit and got that first marvelous view of New Mexico on the other side, I felt sure that the life of man and the existence of the planet were everlasting and glorious, as the universe is.

Raton itself is a northern city, American, unadobe, with a good feeling to it, but it does not make me feel what to me is New Mexico. But the vast earth in which Raton is set is pure New Mexico, with the peculiar blending of starkness and softness which is typical of the earth of this southwestern world. Once out of the city limits there is no mistaking where you are. To the south there is a form rising up from the plain, a mountain like a pyramid, which proclaims New Mexico so marvelously that it might stand for the entire state. As you drive along, this huge form with its massive base and regular slopes remains in view until you are far past Raton, a signal of the tremendous country you have come to.

Not many miles out of Raton the pavement ends. If you connect paved roads with civilization, you may say that not many miles out of Raton civilization ends. However this may be, it is true that you are leaving the world dominated by the forms and forces of Anglo-Saxon America, you are entering the world of America wherein Spanish, Mexican, and Indian influences predominate in all fields except business, banking, and the professions.

You pass through the ranch country of Cimarron. You pass through beautifully wooded Cimarron Canyon. You mount high and sweep down, eagle-like, around Eagle Nest Lake. You dip and glide through Moreno Valley, with high bald or wooded mountains on all sides. You climb to the last pass you have to cross before reaching Taos. You wind down the canyon. Suddenly you come out—as from a narrow passage, as from a tunnel—and there spreads vast Taos Valley, rimmed by near and far distant mountains. And now you are in the land of adobe.

The earth is not red. It has not the sun and fire in it of the earth around Española and Santa Fe. There are no stark sculptured cliffs, no orphaned mesas. It is earth covered by a green wash, suggesting northern country, suggesting Colorado more than the blazing sun-baked country of the true Southwest. Yet here authentically is the world of adobe, of Indian kivas and Mexican *moradas*.

On emerging from the canyon, one of the first adobe houses you see is our house, right near the canyon on US Highway 64, into Taos. It is a neat little house, freshly gone over because of the recent torrents which fell upon the valley and washed earth back to earth, threatening to reduce the region of Taos to a site of adobe ruins—and I may add that no other building becomes a ruin so rapidly as adobe when abandoned. To the average tourist passing along the highway, our house would be indistinguishable from the Mexican houses round about. Your average tourist—he who now at this instant whizzes by—would not dream that none other than Tom Elliot sits herein, pounding the typewriter to his friend Bob.

We arrived yesterday afternoon and have been here not yet twenty-four hours. I've hardly been out, except to snatch Betty off the road. But from previous visits to the general region of Taos and to this neck particularly, I know something of our general surroundings.

We are, I'd judge, about four miles from Taos Plaza. Next to us, in the direction of town, is a small field. Next to this field is an auto camp. Feature Tom and Grace living on the highway in a native house a stone's throw from an auto camp! In no other place would we do it. And, I might add, in no other place could it be done as it is done here. This country is so great that it reconciles everything. It is so vast that it absorbs everything, impressing upon each individual place, no matter how individual and different from the others, a common factor. This given auto camp is, in reality, quite near; yet it seems distant, miles and miles away; indeed it seems not to exist as an auto camp at all. It too is but wood and adobe. The rear ends of cars sticking out from their sheds seem altogether out of place—yet, on second thought, even these units of shaped metal are so covered with dust and mud that they, too, have at least an adobe veneer.

Below the auto camp, if I remember rightly, is a barroom and dance hall, a center of nightlife for the native youths. Further along is one of those atrocities to be met occasionally down here, a discolored pretentious house built by people who had no feeling for this country, its materials and forms. Then come more auto camps, better ones. Then you enter the village of Taos, incorporated.

Somewhere in that village is Grace, shopping while I sit here and pound away.

Do we like it? Of course we do, that's why we came. Are we going to like it? It seems reasonably sure. I will admit, however, that it seemed considerably more sure when we were in New York. In New York, fed up with complexities, the simplicity we would have here seemed too good to be true. There, a large if not elaborate establishment. Here a simple one-story, three-room house. There, three telephones. Here, not one. There, two bathrooms. Here, only a single tap over the kitchen sink and an outdoor privy. There, people to do our house and kitchen work. Here, all the work to do ourselves. In prospect it seemed surely delightful. Just because it was an extreme contrast to all we had been having, we leapt at it. But now that we've landed, I'm not so sure. But perhaps this is only because the place was still upset and unready for us when we arrived, with men tamping on the roof and particles of mud falling down. Or perhaps it is because these small rented quarters remind me and rebuke me for not having a place of our own down here. (Grace and I will begin looking for land at once.) Or perhaps it is because I had a restless time of it last night. Or, lastly, perhaps because I could do no work this morning, and, instead, began writing this letter to you.

Yes, Bob, I must confess that this letter with all its length is but a substitute for my real work. Could I have worked on the book, I'd not have pounded this off to you—even though I did start it two nights ago in a hotel in Pueblo.

Well, let's see. I began by saying that to motor across the continent is to let the physical world into you, with consequent displacement of your ego, your feelings and consciousness of self. It now seems to me that I have demonstrated it. Hardly a word in this letter directly about myself. Most of the words about things seen and physical events. The world of the earth is in me (my subjective world is displaced), and I am not myself.

Yours,

Tom

I cannot end this letter without one last word about mud. Mud, my dear Bob, exists in three conditions. There is mud in its place, as on a river bottom or in a field—in which case it is neither more nor less than plain mud. There is mud shaped and utilized by man, as in this adobe house—in which case it is quite beautiful. There is mud [out of]* place, as I saw it after the floods of Nebraska and Colorado—in which case it is frightful. It is doubtful that you can glean any instruction from this three-fold classification, yet I felt impelled to formulate it.

8

The Elliot living room. Five o'clock the same afternoon. A whiskey bottle and glasses have been set out on Tom's *worktable. The door is open. Voices are heard outside.* Tom *and* Grace *enter with* Lillian Range *and* Bill Bryne.

Lillian Range *is of medium height. Her slender, frail-looking body obeys her. She is dressed in a serviceable grey cloth suit which seems to have been bought for its usefulness rather than because it specially suited her. Her physical wants are few, so that, though she has but little money, she somehow manages to get along. Drinks are the only thing her body seems to like, wine and strong tea. She likes whiskey, but it does not like her. Her black hair, streaked with gray, is parted in the middle and pulled down so that, simple, somewhat severe, almost nunlike, it makes an oval frame for her face.*

Looked at practically, she seems in perpetual poverty. Looked at spiritually, she seems in perpetual wealth. She has some little vanities about her body which surprise you until you get used to them——wants to look sunburned, wants to look well. Overgenerous in her estimates of people, even those whom she does not like. Speaks as if it were her right to speak authoritatively. Takes it well, but really does not like to be disputed or crossed.

* of out

Her age is indeterminate. Fifteen years ago she looked much as she looks today. Mature when quite young, she is still youthful and mature. When she smiles she lights up in a most lovely way, as if all life were morning and she was just awakening to it. In repose, she shows fatigue and strain. At all times she is poised. If she feels pain she never shows it. When she enters the conversation, she lights up and is a vivid participant at once, and confident that what she says is important. At once eager, grave; when silent, she bends her head and seems to be in the room, in the world itself, alone. Sometimes even when talking she seems silent. She speaks with precision, quietly. Sometimes her voice is almost inaudible, as if she has insufficient energy with which to give it body and project it. Invariably she evokes deference and respect. In a subtle way she is usually the center of attention of any group.

Bill Bryne* *is a tall and well-set-up young man with an agreeable, attractive personality. He wears blue jeans, Indian moccasins, a white shirt with an open collar. By any standards he is good looking, with an intelligent forehead and clear humorous eyes. He is direct and candid. By type, he is bound to be popular, in demand for parties of all kinds. However, there is a quizzical critical aloof strain in him which puzzles people and sets him a bit off. He likes his food and his drinks. Without being able to explain the impression, there is something about him which makes the sensitive person aware that he may do the unexpected thing. He is a rover, and so, he is somewhat undependable. He is also loyal, can be loyal, and once he forms a real and deep attachment he can be relied upon to fulfill the friendship and do everything in his power for his friend. He is much more reliable as a friend than as a lover, but as he wants to remain unattached and unobligated, and as he knows he is likely to become obligated through loyalty to a friendship, he tries to keep all of his relationships on a casual basis. He is sensitive, indecisive, has some measure of the feminine in him, likes to be gay, wants some means of serious expression, yet he covers all of this over with an attitude which seems to say, "Life is amusing. I am young and happy-go-lucky and life amuses me."*

He takes things easily, can get along anywhere. He meets life with a mixture of casualness,

* Toomer, *Drama of the Southwest*, holograph, 916.25, has an additional long description of Bryne. It reads:

> BB–
>
> He is a large fair-haired fellow, well put together yet somewhat loose jointed. Seated at table, his legs and feet seem to occupy all the space thereunder. Instead of handing you cigarettes, he will flip them at you. Somewhat of a smart aleck. Now and again he will lean on your shoulder, not out of fondness but as if he meant you to see that in his life you are but a convenient post. His eyes are unexpected. The proportions of his face are generous, but his eyes are set close together, and sometimes there is a piggish glitter in them which suggests that he is conceited and thinks only of himself. His body is sufficient, his mind is alert, his emotions are weak.

criticism, and amusement. In a restrained way, he always seems to be seeing something to laugh at. He has a way of making people wonder as to what's in him, what he has been and done, what he will amount to. Too forthright and obvious to be a man of mystery, he nevertheless keeps a veil over his past acts and says nothing of his hopes for the future. Only to Lillian Range *has he really talked. Between them is some special understanding. She evokes, and he gives her, his very best side.*

BRYNE: We passed the house and next thing I knew we were in the canyon.

ELLIOT: I saw you passing. I called, but you were going too fast. That car of yours seems to have been through things.

BRYNE: It has. I bought it two years ago in Arizona. Took me to Mexico City. Brought me up here. Has never been washed or repaired. All I've done is feed it gas and oil.

ELLIOT: A good advertisement for Plymouth.

GRACE: (*to* Lillian) You will have tea, won't you, my dear?

LILLIAN: If you please. Strong tea.

ELLIOT: No snake medicine?

LILLIAN: Not today, thank you Tom.

Grace *goes to the kitchen and presently returns with a tea tray and buttered crackers.* Elliot *pours drinks for three.*

LILLIAN: Where is Betty? Is she well? I'm so anxious to see her.

GRACE: She's over there somewhere, with her gang, as Tom calls it. I'll go find her before you leave.

ELLIOT: Did it rain in town?

BRYNE: Only a few drops.

ELLIOT: We had it heavy for a while here. It swept over those hills and charged upon us and you couldn't see a thing for a while. Now, you'd hardly know it. Not a cloud in the sky. The earth seems as dry as if it had never rained.

LILLIAN: (*looking around*) I like this room very much. It has good proportions. And what a lovely view. Is that Taos Mountain you see? You will be able to work here, Tom. I feel sure you will.

ELLIOT: Hope so. Didn't go so well this morning.

LILLIAN: It may take several weeks. Only last week I started work, but I'm so happy because I finished a poem this morning. I read it to Grace.

ELLIOT: Read it to me.

LILLIAN: I started to bring it. Then I left it home. You are working better now, aren't you, Bill?

BRYNE: At the kind of thing I do.

LILLIAN: *(to* Grace *and* Tom*)* He wants to write a novel but he has to do what the magazines want.

GRACE: *(to* Lillian*)* What's this about your going to Santa Fe? Are you set and determined? Suppose we find you a better place in Taos?

LILLIAN: I must, my dear. I only waited here because I wanted to see you and Tom.

ELLIOT: What's the matter? You don't like Taos? What a way to treat us—leave just when we arrive.

BRYNE: I keep telling her she won't like Santa Fe as well. I stayed there three days. Three days were enough. The people down there dress up and make a city of it—and they shouldn't. I saw more drunken parties—

ELLIOT: That's exactly what the Santa Fe people say when they come up here—more drunken parties in Taos.

BRYNE: They may say it, but it isn't so. They haven't that kind of money here. The second night I was in Santa Fe I was invited out to a place, not because they knew or liked me—I'd hardly met my hosts—but because there is a scarcity of single men. What I didn't see at that party. I'm a puritan myself, but when you see one man wander off and step off a cliff twenty feet high and land on his feet unhurt and come back to the party still drunk as he was, and when you see couples go in the stream with their clothes on—which wasn't the main idea at all—and when you are criticized for not being drunk enough—

LILLIAN: *(smiling)* Well, I'm not a single young man, and I won't be in demand for those kind of parties. *(To* Elliot, *with a certain reluctance to talk about it, yet impelled to talk because Taos and its experiences are so vivid in her.)* Yes, I like Taos. There is a greatness in these mountains. But I feel a tension in the people. You won't get it out here. You are fortunate you are out of town. I have not met everybody. I like some of them very much, but if you live in town as I do, you become involved, you make the mistake of inviting people who hate each other to the same tea, you get drawn into their quarrels. I've been through all I want.

ELLIOT: Have you met Martha?*

LILLIAN: I haven't. I don't want to. Several people offered to take me to see her, but from all I've heard she is not a woman I want to know.

ELLIOT: And that's that. You are right, but I should also tell you that you are missing something. She'd be an unusual figure anywhere. Here . . . to know her is to know Taos.

GRACE: One aspect of Taos.

ELLIOT: Yes, one aspect only.

LILLIAN: The aspect I've seen too much of, already. You know her, don't you Tom?

ELLIOT: Yes, I do. She regards this region as her domain, you know. Since I am not here under her auspices, I'll be in disfavor. She resents Grace because Grace has individuality.

LILLIAN: But doesn't she invite unusual women to her house?

ELLIOT: Indeed she does. Celebrated men and remarkable women. But in the case of the women it invariably happens this way. She invites them. She gives them no rest until they come. They arrive. Soon she gets angry or jealous or both. Then she is impatient to be rid of the very people she was impatient to have come. With men she is better. She really knows how to treat genius, but her moods and her inordinate desire to play one man against another get the better of her.

LILLIAN: What is she really like? I hear so much; so little is reliable.

BRYNE: A feudal lord, if you ask me. With all of her houses and serfs and vassals. You watch her and you realize what money can do—one woman with money in a poor community. Everybody is at her beck and call.

ELLIOT: Not only because she has money.

* As Toomer edits his holograph, this line serves as an insertion point for the next 1,300 words of dialog. In one of two renderings, it is written, "Have you meet M.L.?" Lillian originally began to share her experiences with Dr. Bright (who appears to be based upon Dr. Light, with whom the poet Lola Ridge stayed in 1935) immediately after discussing local quarrels.

LILLIAN: Then because of what, Tom? What is her influence?

ELLIOT: *(as reluctant to speak of* Martha *as* Lillian *was to speak of Taos, yet, like her, impelled to talk)* There's no mystery about it—or perhaps there is. She's magnetic and unscrupulous.

GRACE: Not magnetizing to me.

BRYNE: Nor to me.

ELLIOT: *(to* Grace*)* You are a woman. *(to* Bryne*)* You are not a celebrity.

LILLIAN: Isn't there a story that she feared the Indians were putting a spell on her, and she went to a psychologist?

ELLIOT: That's the story. It may be true. It may be just another Taos story. If true, imagine it—*she*, fearing the Indians were putting a curse on her. *(to* Lillian*)* You know what Russell Lyndham called her? She got him out here, as she has lured others. Modest lady. She wanted him to write a book about her. After ten days of mutual abnormality, he said she was the symbol of evil, and that if he could kill her he'd destroy all the evil in the world.

BRYNE: How did she like that?

ELLIOT: Enjoyed it, I imagine. Let's give her her due, however. She has brought more people to Taos than all the rest of the people put together. She has the right idea for this country—build an oasis and populate it.

LILLIAN: Is she lonely? Is that it?

BRYNE: Frustrated.

ELLIOT: Both, and much more. She has a mania to control the lives of others. She has some good impulses, she can do large things in a large way, make gestures that are magnificent really—

GRACE: For whom?

ELLIOT: For herself, without doubt. She never loses sight of the figure she cuts. Even so, she can be majestic, sometimes.

GRACE: She wants to be some great man's inspiration.

ELLIOT: Not being, she has turned matriarch with a vengeance. You know, don't you, Bryne, that we live in a matriarchy here?

Bryne *sort of squirms, but says nothing.*

GRACE: Tom has said that before. He has pointed to what he calls the predominance of dominant women here in Taos and in Santa Fe. What I can't get from him is how Taos or Santa Fe differs in this respect from the rest of the country.

ELLIOT: If you will pardon the language, I've even ventured to say that if any man were to marry any one of certain women I have in mind, he would at that instant lose both balls.

GRACE: Tom!

Elliot *and* Bryne *have a laugh.* Lillian *smiles, showing that she can take it.*

ELLIOT: *(sobering)* This is dangerous ground. Only less dangerous than the slopes of Taos. Lillian, you began to tell us about your experiences.

LILLIAN: It has been interesting. I've gained a great deal. I wouldn't give it up for anything. But I feel a tension in the people. I don't know what it is. They can't live alone, because the country dwarfs them. They can't live together—

ELLIOT: Because they feel they are living only when they exert their will on someone else. They are inbred and ingrown. It's the sort of involuntary destructivity you'd get among a handful of people thrown together on a desert island or in a small boat on the ocean.

LILLIAN: But men have been heroic under such conditions.

ELLIOT: Yes, when there was a recognized master of them, when this master was coordinating and directing every ounce of their energies toward the attainment of a purpose as basic as that of survival. Here there is no master-hand, unless it be that of Martha. Here there is no vital purpose.

LILLIAN: Now I think you have put your finger on it. These people have no common purpose. Some number of them are here because of force of circumstance. Like myself, they came here to cure lung trouble. They have made the best of it. Some few have done admirably well, but the reason for their presence in the Southwest is never forgotten and it makes them restless. They feel uprooted, and what is more they never will be rooted here. Their centers—if they have any, if they have any left—are elsewhere. Some of them as individuals have integrity, but collectively—if you can use such a word in relation to them—they have no social conscience, no group feeling or group consciousness. It may be that this is not their country, but the land of the dark-skinned people. It may be that it will take several generations, the children growing up and knowing no other place as home. I could never live here. If this were the only place on Earth in which I would be cured I'd rather burn up.

ELLIOT: I don't feel it so strong as that.

GRACE: To hear you talk, one wouldn't know it.

ELLIOT: No, today I've expressed one side only. There is the other strongly attractive side.

GRACE: I'd like to hear you talk of it sometimes.

LILLIAN: I wonder if you'll ever be happy in Taos, even with a place of your own.

ELLIOT: I wonder too, but it seems we are under a compulsion to try and put it to the test of actual experience. All other places seem tame, humdrum, unadventurous. Ours is the lure of the Southwest. We are under its spell; I always try to see what is possible, what's for me.

LILLIAN: No one could help being drawn to the country. I come back to the people.

BRYNE: *(somewhat crudely to Elliot, his curiosity and smart-aleckness getting the better of his sensitivity of Lillian)* If you don't mind my asking, have you TB?

ELLIOT: No.

BRYNE: Then perhaps you can't answer my question.

ELLIOT: What is it?

BRYNE: Do you think there is a TB psychology, an emotional condition, an attitude to life produced by tuberculosis?

ELLIOT: It's possible, but I can't say.

BRYNE: Might it not explain what you and Lillian seem to feel about the people? And if it does, then I'd say that Santa Fe would be worse than Taos. None of the people I know here have TB. In Santa Fe the woods are full of them.

ELLIOT: *(shrugging and wanting to change the conversation)* It may be.

BRYNE: I wonder how I'd feel if I were held to one place by a disease.

ELLIOT: I wonder.

LILLIAN: (*to* Grace, *somewhat drawn and pale*) May I have another cup of tea, my dear?

Grace *rises at once and goes out for more hot water. The others are uncomfortably silent.* Bryne, *suddenly realizing he has put* Lillian *under stress, is most uncomfortable.*

LILLIAN: (*to* Elliot, *after she has been served tea*) Did Grace tell you of my experiences with Dr. Bright?

ELLIOT: She didn't.

LILLIAN: Dr. Bright is a splendid person and I have nothing but admiration for her. I was staying at her house when the torrents fell. We went through the deluge together. The roof leaked and for several days we lived under umbrellas. Then we could stand it no longer and moved to the Inn. Finally I had to leave her for reasons better left unmentioned. I still think she is a splendid character, on call to every person in the valley, working single-handed, building up a clinic for the Mexicans. But if you stay with a person here and then leave her, everyone begins talking. The less they know, the more they invent. They have invented so much that the wonder is that Dr. Bright and myself are not enemies now. Everything is so personal here. Happenings are exaggerated and distorted and passed around and around until you feel you are in a web.

GRACE: It sounds strange to me. I've never experienced it in Taos.

ELLIOT: That's because you lived near the pueblo, had some share of the Indian life, and kept clear of just the people Lillian is talking about.

GRACE: It may be.

LILLIAN: Oh, I'm sure it is. Grace, you don't know Taos. There is something very disturbing here. From the day I arrived I've never felt settled. After my experience with Dr. Bright I went to the Marshall house. It was worse. With Dr. Bright I was at least out of town. In the Marshall house I was right in it. My room was damp and gloomy.

GRACE: Damp?

LILLIAN: Yes, damp.

ELLIOT: Did you see any black widows?

LILLIAN: We killed a spider on the wall one night. It was large and black, but I'm not sure it was a merry widow.

ELLIOT: *(laughing)* Merry widow—that's a nice name for the ladies.

LILLIAN: Then another night a spider came down on a thread from the ceiling. I went toward it with a piece of paper to take it out. It made a motion toward me, and I had to kill it.

ELLIOT: *(after a glance at the ceiling of this room)* Did it have a shiny black body shaped like part of an hourglass and a red marking?

LILLIAN: I'm not sure. It may have had.

BRYNE: *(to* Elliot*)* Ever seen a centipede? I want to see one. I hear they are around here.

LILLIAN: Are they poisonous?

ELLIOT: Somewhat, but not dangerous like your merry widows. Unpleasant things to see. Bill Bryne, what do you think of Taos?

BRYNE: *(after a pause, with a smile)* I find it very peaceful.

ELLIOT: Peaceful! Do you mean it? That's the very last word I'd use.

BRYNE: I really do. There's something about these slopes, this green valley and the way it is high and surrounded. It's pastoral, that's how Taos strikes me. It's the most peaceful place I've ever been in. I love it.

ELLIOT: Lillian, aren't you amazed?

GRACE: I'm not. I've always had just that feeling, though I'd say it was exciting too.

BRYNE: I agree. It is exciting, but more than anything else I feel a restfulness, a great repose. The days are exciting. When night comes—

ELLIOT: When night comes, the ghosts of a million ancient people, some massacred and murdered, float through the air and weigh upon the living, and for these green slopes which seem so lovely and peaceful to you, it is just in them that something ominous lies. Just in them is the strange oppression and disquiet of Taos. The mountains are magnificent. The valley, at least certain parts of it, has in truth the pastoral quality you feel. But the slopes . . . they seem—how shall I say it? Slippery is the only word that comes. When I get out in the valley, see the towns dotted here and there, and see those slopes to the encircling hills and mountains, I feel we are trapped on an ocean bed, the continents of men rising up high all around us, but we [are] unable to climb up and out because at each attempt our feet slip on the slopes. Time and again we try and slip back. Each frustration makes us more cruel. Thus, though we share a common plight, we are goaded to turn upon and rend each other.

GRACE: Tom, since when have you had such feelings? I've never heard you express them before.

ELLIOT: It would seem that all sorts of things are coming to the surface. No, I haven't expressed them before. But you have heard me say that all this country gives me the impression of being underwater. Do you feel that, Lillian? In this stark dry country, I feel the presence of water. Every time I look at the mountains, I feel them submerged—the cloud effects, the shadows, the patches of sea green, the way the sun filters through, as if it were coming down through water.

BRYNE: Isn't it true that they've found seashells in some of the cliffs?

ELLIOT: I've heard tell. In my mind there is no doubt that all of it was once under water. I'm sure of it. I'm sure, for example, that many of those [sculpted]* forms we see and wonder at, like those of the region just before you pass Española on the road to Taos, were modeled by the original waters as they rushed off when the land began rising from an ocean bed to its present elevation. There they've been standing ever since, ancient relics of the great wash, not caused by the slow erosion of wind and rain and the lesser washes. I'm geologically unsound, in all probability; but these are my humble if fanciful thoughts about it.

LILLIAN: Tom is right. There is a cruelty here. It is a land of blood and devotion. The Indians and Mexicans know how to live in it. White people, with no religion and no devotion, become cruel only.

BRYNE: *(with a smile)* I can see what you mean, but I honestly don't feel that at all. I've never met kinder or softer people than these Mexicans. Their voices are a bit harsh, but what of it. They are supposed to be cruel to animals; I've never seen an example of it. The Penitentes may flagellate themselves, but they are damned decent to you and me. I confess to not knowing much about the Indians, but I like those I've seen. The people of our own kind here are as pleasant to be with as any I've found anywhere.

* Word obscure.

All sorts of things go on, but don't they go on everywhere?

ELLIOT: You are lucky to be able to take Taos so casually and physically.

BRYNE: Physically? How do you mean?

ELLIOT: You meet it with your body. You have a young healthy body with no bothersome nerves. You drive your car. You eat well and sleep well. The human discords amuse you. The psychological and superphysical factors sort of roll off your back. You have no family. You look at this place with the eyes of a visiting rover. You are free to pick up and leave when you wish. You aren't thinking of buying land, building a house, and settling here. You are young and having a good time. You haven't tried to climb one of those slopes. Taos hasn't really entered you.

BRYNE: You may be right. I've never wanted to settle anywhere.

LILLIAN: He is right, Bill. There are things he doesn't know about you, but all Tom said was right. I'd be happy here if I could take it physically, if I had a car and could get out in the country.

GRACE: Haven't you been? Haven't you been out? There are such marvelous things to see. Tom and I will take you. You must see the land we are thinking of buying.

ELLIOT: There are marvelous things to see. There's one place I've never been, and it fascinates me. Blue Lake—up on the other side of the sacred mountain. There the Indians have dances which no white man has ever seen.

LILLIAN: I'd love to go. How far is it?

GRACE: That's hardly a trip for you. It's twenty or thirty miles from the pueblo. You have to walk or take a horse a good part of the way. I've never been. You can reach it, I've been told, from Twining—which itself is not an easy trip. The Indians go up the canyon directly north of the pueblo, and reach Blue Lake that way. You've been out to the pueblo, haven't you?

LILLIAN: No, I haven't.

GRACE: You must go there.

ELLIOT: Let's go tonight. We'll go tonight and hear the singing.

LILLIAN: I'd love to.

GRACE: Every night the boys sing. There are three bridges over the stream. A group stands on each bridge. When I lived near there, I heard them every night. All is dark, except for a few lights from the pueblo houses on both sides of the creek. The dark mountain looms up in the background. All is still. Then the singing begins.

ELLIOT: We'll go tonight. Tomorrow we'll go other places, show Lillian that proposed land of ours.

LILLIAN: I'd like to see that land. It will be fine to go around with you. I leave Taos in three days.

ELLIOT: Three days?

GRACE: You can't. Won't you stay if we find you a better place?

LILLIAN: I'm sorry, dear, but I must've had all I can stand. These last three days with you will be my vacation. Then I must get some work done. I feel I'll be able to work in Santa Fe.

ELLIOT: What's this we hear about Mexico?

LILLIAN: I'd like to go there in two months. I want to economize now, so as to make the trip possible.

ELLIOT: Mexico, in August?

LILLIAN: Mexico at any time of the year. There is something there for me. I feel it. I've always wanted to go. Having seen New Mexico, I want to see Old Mexico all the more.

ELLIOT: Suicide.

LILLIAN: No, Tom. If you do what you need to do, you may meet death but it is not suicide. What time is it now?

BRYNE: After six.

LILLIAN: *(rising)* We must go.

ELLIOT: What for? Stay and have dinner with us and then we'll go to the pueblo.

9

Taos Pueblo. Night in the Southwest, luminous dark, the stars accessible, almost within reach. The black form of Taos Mountain lifts skyward behind the pueblo. The slope to the south is broken by Pueblo Canyon, then the hills continue around. The terraced six-storied pueblos on either side of the creek are themselves like dark hills, except that lamps burning in several of the houses identify them as human habitations. All is still. In this dark night the pueblo seems to expand, loom, blend with its setting, and be immeasurable. The stranger has no means of knowing the extent of the space between the two main buildings. The only sound heard is the running of the stream. Now and again the shadowy form of an Indian, blanket around his head, passes silently across the plaza.

Four dark figures enter, trying to walk as silently as the Indians. Chary of speech, when they do talk, they speak in whispers. No cigarettes are lighted.

ELLIOT: How's this for a place?

GRACE: Good. The stream and the three bridges are just over there.

Tom *and* Grace *spread blankets on the ground. The group settles down, listening, expectant, no one speaking for a while.*

GRACE: Are you warm enough?

LILLIAN: Yes, thank you, dear. Where are we?

GRACE: In the middle of the plaza. Horses and wagons and the cars of tourists pass right along here in the daytime. That's the south pueblo in front of you. That's the north pueblo behind.

LILLIAN: Are they far separated?

GRACE: Not far.

LILLIAN: I wouldn't know how long I'd have to walk to reach that building. How beautiful they are! I know they are beautiful by my feeling.

GRACE: You must see them in daylight too. We'll bring you out to see Adam. He's our friend. I won't take you now because I never go to their houses after sundown unless especially invited.

LILLIAN: They go to sleep early?

GRACE: Sometimes. Sometimes they sing into all hours of the night.

LILLIAN: Are these their houses in these two large buildings?

GRACE: Yes, their houses.

LILLIAN: All of them occupied? You don't see anyone, do you? If it weren't that I feel the presence of life, I would think we were out in the mountains or in a prehistoric village.

GRACE: Most of them. Some of the interior rooms are dark. They're built around them. These are vacant or used as storerooms. All the others are occupied.

LILLIAN: It is amazing. You see nothing; you feel everything. I've never felt the presence of life so keenly, in no city, in no community anywhere. This place is lived in, it is inhabited. It is a real community. It is communal, isn't it?

GRACE: Yes, it is.

LILLIAN: How many people are there?

GRACE: About 500.

ELLIOT: Think of the task facing modern society. To make a community out of the world's millions of peoples.

BRYNE: Hopeless.

LILLIAN: They are doing it in Russia, Bill.

BRYNE: I'm not so sure. This place grew, and it took centuries to grow. Over there in the Soviets they are trying to manufacture something in a few years. It can't be done.

ELLIOT: Whether possible or not, it is absolutely necessary that we attempt it. The whole world needs a new automatism.

BRYNE: A new automatism? What is that?

ELLIOT: Too long to go into now. These Indians have an automatic society which functions. The rest of the world—most of it—is breaking up, running irregularly or not at all. We are searching and revolting and fighting for a new way in which to function automatically, just as these Indians now do and we have done for ages. Communism, for example, is one of the programs which promises to give modern man a pueblo, a pueblo adapted to his complex needs. But we didn't come out here to talk. Grace, isn't it strange that there's not singing yet?

GRACE: Quite strange.

ELLIOT: What time did we leave the house?

GRACE: Around nine, wasn't it?

LILLIAN: Are we too late?

GRACE: No, it's strange. They sing until eleven or twelve or later.

ELLIOT: Perhaps we are too early.

GRACE: No, that's not it.

Pause, silence, everyone again aware of the pueblo only, all again listening, expectant.

Presently the form of an Indian moves toward them through the darkness. The Indian, an older man, stops. The group, somewhat startled, looks up.

INDIAN: Hello.

ELLIOT: Hello.

INDIAN: Cold tonight.

ELLIOT: Hot today and cold tonight.

INDIAN: Where you from?

ELLIOT: New York. You know about New York? The big city near the ocean.

INDIAN: I know about.

ELLIOT: We come way out here.

INDIAN: Long way.

ELLIOT: Have you seen the ocean?

INDIAN: No. Where you live?

ELLIOT: You mean around here? We have a house on the other side of Taos.

INDIAN: The other side of Taos.

ELLIOT: Yes, just before you enter the canyon on the road to Cimarron.

INDIAN: I know place.

ELLIOT: Will the boys sing tonight?

INDIAN: Sing every night.

ELLIOT: Did we come too late?

INDIAN: No.

ELLIOT: Will they sing later on?

INDIAN: Don't know. The boys sing every night.

ELLIOT: We will wait.

INDIAN: *(moving off)* Goodnight.

ELLIOT: Goodnight.

Pause, silence.

ELLIOT: And now we know as much as we did before. There's something strange about this.

GRACE: (to Lillian) Are you sure you aren't cold? I have another blanket. Do you want to wait?

LILLIAN: I could stay right here all night.

Pause, silence.

ELLIOT: Even the dogs are still.

Pause, silence.

LILLIAN: Where do they dance?

GRACE: Right here, sometimes. In the corn dance they go from house to house all around the pueblo.

LILLIAN: I haven't seen a dance. Do they dance well here?

GRACE: Not as well as at some of the other pueblos.

BRYNE: Everyone says the Domingo corn dance is the one to see.

GRACE: It is intense and beautiful, one of the most impressive, but the tourists spoil it.

LILLIAN: When is it?

BRYNE: August fourth, I believe.

LILLIAN: I'll still be in Santa Fe then. I must see it.

Pause, silence.

LILLIAN: That is Taos Mountain up back there, isn't it?

ELLIOT: The sacred mountain.

LILLIAN: Do they hold ceremonies there?

ELLIOT: I believe so.

GRACE: Yes, they do.

LILLIAN: Do you know what they are and what they mean?

ELLIOT: I'd like to know, but I can't bring myself to ask out of curiosity. They wouldn't tell me anyway. Neither would I, if I were in their place.

LILLIAN: Is Taos an Indian name?

ELLIOT: They say not. It has no place or meaning in their language. Taos isn't their name for the pueblo or for the mountain. The pueblo is called by a name that means Red Willow Creek. They have a marvelous word for the mountain—Mawhaulina*—I don't know what it means, but what a name for that massive elevation.

LILLIAN: Mawhaulina. Yes, that is a great name.

Pause, silence.

LILLIAN: What is that gap to the right of the mountain?

ELLIOT: That opening? That is the canyon to Blue Lake.

LILLIAN: Is it Indian land?

ELLIOT: Legally, and by right of living. For a way up, some of the Indians have fields. There is grazing land for cattle. There is good trout fishing in the stream. Wood and vigas come from there. It is a beautiful canyon. Go up a ways, and you are in mountain country with huge pine trees. You have left adobe, sagebrush, cactus, and the flowers of the badlands behind. You would never know that there was a town called Taos set on a slope of the hills in the blazing sun.

LILLIAN: It sounds wonderful. Is there an Indian name for it?

ELLIOT: Yes, but I don't know what it is. A few miles up there is a lovely natural clearing called Glorietta.† Beyond this is a glade where the Indians sometimes do what we would call picnic, stay there all day, fish, cook over an open fire. This glade, too, has a name. There the road ends. Wagons but not cars can go a distance beyond, deeper and deeper into the forest. Then only horses or men on foot. If you know the way and climb long enough you reach Blue Lake.

LILLIAN: Tom, what is Blue Lake that it fascinates you so?

ELLIOT: I couldn't tell you.

* While more recent sources suggest Mó-ha-loh or Má-ha-lu (*Taos News* 2011), a 1920 article by J. P. Harrington of the Bureau of American Ethnology in *American Anthropologist* on Indian place names renders the word from the Taos dialect as Maqwaluna, the meaning of which was obscure to the ethnologists (353).

† Mabel Dodge Luhan writes of Glorietta in *Winter in Taos* (185).

Pause, silence.

LILLIAN: No singing yet.

GRACE: There must be some reason, but I don't know it. This is most unusual. Perhaps we should wait no longer. If they were going to sing they'd have begun by now.

LILLIAN: Let's wait anyway. I may never have another night like this.

ELLIOT: Not often are we helped to be.

LILLIAN: I feel a great peace here.

BRYNE: You laughed at me when I said Taos was peaceful.

ELLIOT: So I did. I wouldn't have laughed if you had said the pueblo.

GRACE: Now you understand my feeling. It is this I mean when I say Taos.

ELLIOT: Then say pueblo.

Pause, silence.

ELLIOT: Speaking of names, last year Adam told us that the Indians have names for every peak and hill and every special form and location in the entire region, not only just around Taos but as far north as the Colorado border and far south down the Rio Grande. Each Indian name, as we know, has a meaning. To name a thing is to feel familiar with it. Whatever is named is to some degree humanized and included in the human world. To the Indians, then, all of this country is humanized, it is living, it is understood and loved, and it is spiritualized—as most of the names have a religious significance. I've often wondered how it would be to be born into this country as an Indian, to grow up in a New Mexico that your ancestors for centuries back had made their own, a New Mexico not only of earth and men but of the gods. This I would call a legacy. This atmosphere of the peopled and the living. In my mind I am convinced that the planet is a living being, that the entire universe is an organism—but I do not feel it. My orientation, like that of most white men, is mental and practical—with a void where the emotions should be, where *being* should be. The Indian child is born into a living earth, he grows up within a living planet, *feeling* his life and the life of the planet and an intimate connection between the two. We may laugh at what we call his superstitions, but they serve to let him feel—and the feeling itself, not the means of its evocation, is the important thing. He does not laugh at us for the same reason that we do not laugh at those who are destitute. Sometimes, to be sure, he satirizes or caricaturizes our ridiculousness. I've heard of dances that are inimitable burlesques of our doings; but on the whole the Indian does not laugh. The white world comes to him and he pities us. Where else in the world does the conqueror evoke compassion?

BRYNE: He imitates us.

ELLIOT: You mean some wear our kind of clothes, some have motorcars, some buy groceries at a chain store, some hang around Taos Plaza, some few run around after Mexican girls? A skin-deep kind of influence, when you think of what we've tried to do to them, when you think of what they mean to us. We have stolen their lands and given them our religion. We have broken or changed some of their customs and forced them into our schools—but the pueblos still go on, dying perhaps, but spiritually intact, dying as much because of age as because of us, still alive enough to give our boisterous child-active civilization an example of how men behave in a mature society.

BRYNE: You call the Indians mature? They're childish, that's what's the matter with them. They couldn't stand up to us. Every time I talk to an Indian I feel like I'm talking to a ten-year-old.

ELLIOT: What would [you] say is the mark of a child, what [is] the mark of maturity? Many things come to mind. You may not be able to give your best answer offhand. Let me suggest how it seems to me. A child is incessantly active. A child does all sorts of purposeless things. His activity, however, does serve the purpose of growth. All activity is fruitful if it serves growth. Now the people of our civilization are active rather than reflective, wouldn't you say?

BRYNE: I would.

ELLIOT: To this extent, then, they have the mark of a child. Now would you say that we are good children, normal children? Does all of our bustle and to-do serve the purpose of growth? You don't want to answer, but the answer is obvious. We are children—which is all right—but we are children without growing.

BRYNE: Everybody is talking about arrested development.

ELLIOT: That's damning, but even so there just may be some truth to it. To go on. A mature person is contemplative. In him, growth through activity has ceased to be the main way. He is comparatively inactive, therefore. His way is growth through contemplation. Activity builds the body. Contemplation builds the soul. A child is a body without a soul. An adult is a body with a soul forming. On this basis, would you say that as a race we are mature?

BRYNE: I would not.

ELLIOT: Now for the moment forget those accessories of living such as money, banks, policemen, machine guns, commerce, science, armies and navies, sovereign states, wars and revolutions and the like, and focus on just the essential matter of activity with or without growth and contemplation. Are the Indians child-active?

BRYNE: No.

ELLIOT: Are they contemplative?

BRYNE: Don't ask me.

ELLIOT: Neither do I know, but my impression is that they are. I've seen them wrapped in their blankets, sitting on those terraces, watching—what? You or I would be looking at the mountain or at the sunset. They seem to be contemplating not only their individual lives and environment but their entire race history. Only from sculptures of the Buddha have I had such a feeling of contemplative power. The impression is so strong that I'd even say that only among these Indians is the art of contemplation, the greatest of the arts, not lost. Speaking for myself, I am doing my best when, cowlike, I ruminate. An animal ruminates. A man should be able to contemplate.

BRYNE: Then you think we should foreswear our ways and imitate the Indians? It might be fun to go native. I've never tried it. It's your argument. You lead the way.

ELLIOT: I seldom argue. I either know or I don't know. Imitate the Indians? Of course not. We couldn't if we would. I began by saying, if you remember, that the Indians give our boisterous child-active civilization an example of how men behave, how they *be*, in a mature society. An example, a hint of possible dignity. We must be born above the body* in our own way. It is for this hint

* In *From Exile into Being*, the autobiography he worked on from 1937–1946, Toomer repeatedly uses the phrase "born above the body" to describe the 1926 mystical experience on an elevated train platform in New York that left him with feelings of harmony and enlightenment. Toomer, *From Exile into Being*, excerpted as "The Experience," in *Jean Toomer Reader*, ed. Rusch, 33–76.

that we come. This is why we are glad to be sitting at this moment, four orphans of civilization, on the dirt road of a pueblo plaza while the Indians themselves, unmindful and indifferent to us, pursue their unmemorable way of living. Ask yourself this. On what other road would you sit like this, on what other dirt of paved or bejeweled plaza? In what other plaza could you be as we have been tonight? Now you see what I mean. Until you see a star you cannot want it, until you see a man you cannot want to be a man. Until you taste bread you can't want to eat it. There is a leaven here which the more fortunate of us may share and use for our own baking. Seeds for a forgotten field, yeast for forgotten wheat, a promise of harvest for the radiant reaper.

GRACE: Even if no singing tonight.

LILLIAN: If they had sung, we would have heard them. In their silence, we heard ourselves.

GRACE: Shall we go then?

ELLIOT: We'd better. The body is still.

BRYNE: Inactive.

All rise, gather their things, and slowly move off.

ELLIOT: And so we leave the pueblo in its peace to pursue our own less immemorial but equally necessary way of living. Indians of pueblo, you will not hear me, but thank you—and goodnight.

10

Day in the Southwest, blue-brilliant, dazzling. The roof of an adobe house with a weathered ladder leading thereto. The Taos Visionary [Ubeam] *and the* Taos Kid [Buck Fact] *are in their respective places and postures. On the ground directly below the* Visionary *a sheep grazes. Below the* Kid *stands a burro.*

UBEAM: The clouds hold junta over the mountains.

BUCK FACT: You've said that enough. Junta, junta—it's a good word all right, but only the Spanish comrades will understand what you mean, not that it's important. Why speak of clouds? Who cares where they meet? Clouds—as if there weren't a world full of men and plenty to say about them.

UBEAM: As the clouds eschew the valleys in favor of the peaks, giving to the mountains the full force of their rain, thunder, and the three forks of their lightning, so men are magnetized from the lowlands to the high places of the earth. Taos is the American Lhasa. New Mexico is the American Tibet, the vast bright cradle of new world lamas.

BUCK FACT: I don't get you. Are you boosting for our state? Then why drag in lamas and Lhasa and Tibet? That spoils everything. I've read about Tibet. It's the place where a bunch of goofy fellows went to cook up a soul. We don't want that kind around here. They go cuckoo in the end and do devil dances worse than any Apache ever saw. Say Taos is the American Moscow, say New Mexico is the American Soviet, and you will have said something.

UBEAM: The valley is a symbol of contentment. The mountain is a symbol of striving. The pass is for them who have overcome. In New Mexico the mountain men will gather, superb men on the magnificent roof of the world.

BUCK FACT: You *are* boosting for our state, now I'm a New Mexico booster myself. I was born here and I hope to die here when the time comes, die and be buried in a little Mexican cemetery with a red flowerpot tiled over my grave. But let's look at the facts. Where are the great events taking place today? Where are your superb men gathered? Where is your bright cradle of the new world? On housetops? On mountains? On your roof of the world? Not so. There's more happening in Moscow than on all of the mountains of this adobe planet. Your lamas are back numbers. My comrades are the men. New York, Chicago, and San Francisco are close to sea level. Be my witness when I say it, what my comrades in those low cities do will decide the fate of us up here, even if we lived on North Truchas Peak.

11

Taos Plaza. The northwest corner of the plaza, 10 a.m. of a business day. The sun blazes down. As the road is closed because of construction work, no cars are parked at the curbing. Most of the buildings are single-storied adobe. On the north side are a chain grocery store, the Taos variety of a five and ten, and a large vacant store under construction. Here the sidewalk ends. A narrow dirt street shoots off to the north. A similar street shoots off to the west. On this corner is the bank building, also of adobe, but two storied, the upper floor housing the offices of lawyers and the like. From the roof of the bank, four drains project some distance over the streets. On the west side of the plaza are a tavern, a clothing store, a hardware and general store, and J. C. Penney. From the stores an adobe roofing extends to the curb, shading the sidewalk.

It has a bright cheery unhurried atmosphere, this plaza, this commercial center of the entire valley, giving one a feeling that here is a good place to do business, to meet friends, or just to stand around and watch what goes on. There is a continual stream of people going back and forth, stopping to talk, entering and emerging from the stores.

Indians are in the minority, yet they, too, are here, the men with their hair in two braids and a cloth around their middle, the women wearing white buckskin moccasins with the several folds which cause them to walk in their characteristic way. A man and his wife enter the chain store. An older man sort of lopes along, bearing a heavy sack on his back. Two young men stand smoking, one in a doorway, one leaning against a post. Several stroll by, as if in the plaza simply to see the sights and mingle with the crowd of all types and descriptions.

Mexicans are here. Most of the young fellows are dressed in dark trousers and brilliant blue shirts. One wears white trousers and fancy shoes. One or two are in regulation conventional day suits, coat and all. These latter are businessmen, or have employment in municipal or county offices, Taos being a county seat and employing more Mexicans than Anglos.

There is a sprinkling of ranchmen and cowboys with their five-gallon hats and high-heeled boots. There are the native whites of the village, children, young men and young ladies, adults, businessmen, housewives. Most of these dress simply and conventionally. There are the summer visitors, most of them attired, according to their individual ideas and tastes, in outfits suited to summer in New Mexico. There are those who live in or near Taos permanently and belong to the art-intellectual group. The majority of these favor blue jeans and blue work shirts, pale and soft from many washings.

Then, last but not least, are the tourists—they of recent arrival and soon departure. Dressed in all manner of garb—dusty trousers, wilted shirts, sun suits, jodhpurs, linen suits, sharp urban apparel—they are distinguishable from all the others by the sort of nervous curiosity which lays hold of our countrymen when they are sighting and seeing what they believe to be exotic.

The crowd accumulates. The crowd thins out.

On the shaded sidewalk of the north side of the plaza, three people stand talking. Though they block the way, the passerby does not mind. Unhurried, leisurely, good natured, indifferent, the crowd drifts around them as it will have to drift around other stationary groups. These three people are the Tough Girl [Hanna Gow] *and the two* Landladies. *The* Landladies, *wearing their usual blue jeans, are animated and voluble, voices pitched a bit high.* Hanna Gow, *in her usual blue jeans and high-heeled boots, is characteristically brief-spoken and hardboiled.*

HANNA: Are the lord and lady settled? Their arrival is the latest gossip about town.

FIRST LANDLADY: Just about. We finished this morning—all but a few odds and ends. We have a new inventory to make—

HANNA: Are they known to walk off with things?

FIRST LANDLADY: Oh, no. It's just that we like to give our tenants a list of household things and keep a copy for ourselves. It saves trouble at the end, in case the question comes up of what belongs to whom.

HANNA: Have they paid the rent?

FIRST LANDLADY: Grace Elliot sent me a check from New York.

HANNA: Noble of her.

FIRST LANDLADY: We asked for it. The extra expense of the roof—

HANNA: Quite right. People with money usually pay their bills a year late and wonder why business is bad.

SECOND LANDLADY: You should have seen Mr. Elliot dance.

HANNA: Dance? What do you mean?

SECOND LANDLADY: He did an Indian dance and got us to dance with him.

HANNA: Tom Elliot, that distinguished gentleman? Sure he didn't talk about it? Was he drunk?

SECOND LANDLADY: He'd just gotten up.

HANNA: Grace has been teaching him to love the Indians.

FIRST LANDLADY: We must be off.

HANNA: What's the rush?

FIRST LANDLADY: A few things to buy for the house.

HANNA: It's furnished, isn't it? (I thought it was furnished.)

FIRST LANDLADY: We don't see why she wants a new bread box, but the house does need a garbage can that the dogs can't get into. We meant to buy one before they came.

HANNA: What else? You spoil them. I ought to be the landlord.

FIRST LANDLADY: An ironing board.

HANNA: Don't tell me Grace Elliot is going to wash and iron.

FIRST LANDLADY: Someone is. Clean clothes for a child are a problem.

HANNA: She's cute, that child with those large dark eyes of hers. If I saw her enough I might even come to like the parents.

FIRST LANDLADY: *(moving off)* You are coming to us this evening, aren't you?

HANNA: Much of a party?

FIRST LANDLADY: People to meet Harold Vines. Nothing extra.

HANNA: Have you asked your new tenants?

FIRST LANDLADY: Why, no. We didn't think of them. They don't go out much when they're here.

HANNA: The one good thing about them. Yup, I'll be there. Expect me late.

The Landladies *mingle with the crowd and soon disappear in the door of the general store.* Hanna Gow *is about to stroll in the same direction when* Bill Bryne *comes up behind her, touching her on the shoulder.*

HANNA: So it's you, Mr. Bryne.

BRYNE: Formal this morning, aren't you?

HANNA: Formal last night, weren't you?

BRYNE: Lillian took me out to meet the Elliots.

HANNA: And you couldn't get away.

BRYNE: That's it.

HANNA: Suddenly weak. Too much sun? Too much altitude? What are you going to blame?

BRYNE: Suddenly weak—but you're the only one who's discovered it. What's new?

HANNA: Not a thing.

BRYNE: Nothing new in New Mexico?

HANNA: If that's the best you can do after an evening with the Elliots I'd advise you to soak in a nightclub for a month.

BRYNE: Your example is always good.

Hanna *gives him a flash of anger and is about to walk off.*

BRYNE: Hold, lady, hold. Let's straighten out our little affairs.

HANNA: That's simple.

BRYNE: What about the party tonight?

HANNA: What about it?

BRYNE: Do we go?

HANNA: You're asking me?

BRYNE: We had a date, didn't we?

HANNA: Your memory wasn't so good last night. I'm going late.

BRYNE: Suits me. I have dinner with Lillian and the Elliots. Lillian leaves tomorrow.

HANNA: Leaves, tomorrow? I thought she had decided to stay. She's making a mistake.

BRYNE: We agree for once.

HANNA: What's the idea? I like her, but she's a strange one. She economizes here so as to go to Santa Fe. In Santa Fe she'll economize so as to go to Mexico. In Mexico she'll economize so as to return to New York. What's the use of moving around like that? Why doesn't she stay in one place and give herself a chance to live in it?

BRYNE: Live in it? She lives in herself. Wish I could say the same for myself. You make the mistake of all the others around here and think that the only way to live is to have a big house and give parties.

HANNA: I knew Lillian when you were in high school.

BRYNE: I'm a child. I know it. Rub it in. Elliot gave me a lecture last night.

HANNA: Are you driving her?

BRYNE: I don't want to risk the car, with her in it.

HANNA: I'll take her. If she must go, I'm not going to let her go down on the bus.

BRYNE: So the Elliots felt. Yesterday she said she was leaving Thursday. This morning she wants to get away as soon as possible.

HANNA: Why the sudden rush?

BRYNE: She didn't say. The Elliots offered to take her Thursday. Now she wants to see if they can go tomorrow.

HANNA: They never put themselves out for anybody. Tell her I'll take her whenever she wants. That's the least I can do. Look, here comes Martha and the McMasters.

BRYNE: I'm off.

But he doesn't go off.

HANNA: Don't be a fool. I want you to meet her.

BRYNE: I've met her twice already. She doesn't deign to remember me.

HANNA: Haven't you been told that unimportant young men like you must meet her three times? After the third, she'll nod when she passes.

BRYNE: Who gives a damn about her nods?

Martha Coleman *sweeps up. Much in motion when she walks. When she stops she stops dead and stands there solid and immovable. A woman of extremes—a formidable personage, a child, ready to do battle, quick to fly in retreat, courteous and crude, generous and tightfisted, her dominant quality is what may be called hefty femininity. Hefty as any man, she is much the female at the same time. Her stout body is attired in ultra-feminine apparel, expensive, curiously becoming, in good taste yet unexpected on the plaza of Taos. She wears a wide wavy-brimmed summer hat, carries herself with dignity and command, and is without doubt the grand lady of the place.*

On either side of her, yet slightly behind, as if this walk up a sidewalk were a procession in court, are the McMasters, *husband and wife, two among the numbers of* Martha Coleman's *summer guests.*

HANNA: Good morning, Martha. We don't see you on the plaza often these days.

MARTHA: Good morning, [Hanna].* Won't they ever finish the roads?

MRS. MCMASTER: Don't you like it like this? I should think it would be nice if cars were kept out of the plaza all the time.

HANNA: For looks but not for convenience. Oh. Pardon me. Martha, let me introduce Bill Bryne. And Mr. and Mrs. McMaster, this is Bill Bryne.

Martha *gives* Bryne *a blank nod, lowers her eyes, then looks away. Now she is restive, sullen, and petulant that she has been stopped.*

* Holograph reads Lucy.

Bryne *nods to the* McMasters *but can hardly refrain from showing his hostility to* Martha.

MARTHA: We have things to do. Come along, will you, [Hanna]?* I want to speak with you.

The group moves on, leaving Bryne *to trail after, if he will.*

HANNA: *(looking back)* Aren't you coming, Bill?

Bryne *scowls, starts to stride off in the opposite direction and bumps into* Tom Elliot.

ELLIOT: Hello.

BRYNE: Hello.

ELLIOT: But for you, I might have run into the lady herself. Isn't that our matriarch up there?

BRYNE: None other.

Elliot *follows the group with his eyes until they disappear in the bank building.*

[In lost pages of this scene, Bill Bryne *and* Tom Elliot *discuss* Helen *and* John Woodward.*]*

[Bryne] [. . .] involved was not even in town that night or that week. I know this for a fact. †

ELLIOT: Have you said so?

BRYNE: On occasion. They don't want facts. They want scandal.

ELLIOT: Your peaceful little town.

BRYNE: Guess I'll never hear the end of that. Must be a bad day for me. You're the third person in the last half hour to rub it in.

ELLIOT: I'm going out to see John.

BRYNE: You won't find him at his house.

* Lucy

† Bill Bryne seems to be referencing a rumor that an architect named Richard Holt is the father of Helen Woodward's child, and attesting to Holt's absence from Taos at the relevant time. Helen confides to Grace Elliot about this rumor in the next scene.

ELLIOT: No? Do you know where?

BRYNE: He's in his car most of the time, tearing about this peaceful countryside. Saw it parked over there. He may be somewhere around the plaza now.

ELLIOT: Thanks. If you see Lillian and she wants to find us, we'll probably be at the Woodwards'. See! Here comes the parade back.

BRYNE: I'm off.

Elliot follows Bryne's retreat with amused eyes. When he turns around, Martha and her group are almost upon him. He takes the initiative and walks forward to shake hands with her. Martha stops dead. After giving him a limp hand and a vexed begrudged smile she lowers her eyes.

ELLIOT: How are you?

MARTHA: Well enough.

ELLIOT: I heard you were away.

MARTHA: I'm back. You know the McMasters and [Hanna Gow]*, don't you?

ELLIOT: Yes. How do you do? (to Martha) I want to come up and pay my respects.

MARTHA: Better phone before you do. We're busy.

ELLIOT: So am I and I have no phone. Adiós.

He moves on, smiling but smarting from the exchange of slaps. Without a word, without a smile, Martha Coleman strides ahead. Elliot going west, Martha going east. Both seem to rip holes in the plaza crowd.

12

The same morning. The sitting room of the Woodward house. With low ceiling, a southwest fireplace, and yellow-painted walls, it is not unlike the interiors of many other adobe houses except that the furniture is of John's making. Each piece is solid and honest but undistinguished. Each piece is durable but still. It is as if he had worked on them with ideas and hands, leaving both feeling and imagination out—as if he had worked for the sake of occupying himself, not for the sake of those who would occupy the chairs. Helen Woodward and Grace Elliot are in

* Lucy Frisk

the midst of a conversation. Seated near each other they seem strained, partly on account of the chairs. Helen *has her sewing out. She sews as she talks.*

HELEN: Why can't they let me alone? I thought they were my friends. I've never done anything to them.

GRACE: What do you care what they say? Let them say what they will. If you aren't affected, what does it matter what anyone says? It seems to me that your problem is not with them but with yourself.

HELEN: How can you say that? Even if John didn't believe it, who wants such a story hanging over her head? I have to live here. The child is going to grow up here.

GRACE: You say they are talking, they won't leave you alone. Who are *they*, Helen?

HELEN: Everybody.

GRACE: But don't you see, my dear, it can't be. Be specific. Who is talking? It can't be [that] everyone is. I know at least a few of the people of Taos, and I know they are not the kind to spread such a story. If you yourself hadn't told me, I doubt that I would have heard it.

HELEN: Didn't John talk?

GRACE: John? We've only seen him once, and he said nothing about it.

HELEN: Once? Stop lying, Grace. Why can't you tell me the truth? You know he's been with you and Tom constantly since the day you arrived.

GRACE: (*starting to get annoyed*) We've only been here three days.

HELEN: I didn't say anything about that. I said John has been with you constantly.

GRACE: He hasn't. We've seen him once. Most of the time he was talking to Tom. I'm sure he said nothing about you and this story because if he had I'm sure Tom would have told me.

HELEN: You are telling the truth? Then John was lying.

GRACE: Of course I am. Don't let this thing get you. Don't become suspicious of everyone.

HELEN: He said he was seeing you. Where has he been? Just these last few days he is worse. He leaves the house early. I rarely see him at lunch. I may see him at dinner. He says nothing. That awful weight and gloom of him fills the room. He stares at me or ignores me. If he stares I feel he is seeing something contemptible. If he looks away, I feel him accusing me. He is awful to mother. He goes out. I hear him coming back late at night and arranging the chairs in the next room. He'd rather sleep on chairs than in the same bed with an adulterous wife—and it's all a horrid lie.

GRACE: Tell me what happened.

HELEN: Five years ago we spent the summer at Cape Cod. Richard Holt was there. We both liked him, and then John got jealous. Holt left. I didn't see him or hear from him after that. Then suddenly he appeared here at the door. He was passing through Taos, learned that we were living here, and came to say hello. John was out—Mother was out. Naturally I asked him in. He's an architect. It was his first sight of adobe. He was interested in everything. There wasn't much to show, but I took him through the rooms. We were in the bedroom when I heard someone knock. We stepped from the room and there was Nancy Bush in the house. I knew what a gossip Nancy is. I felt funny. I suppose I showed it. And that was all. Even Nancy, herself, made nothing of it until months later when she saw me pregnant. If she'd only count. The child is due this month. Richard Holt was here in November.

GRACE: Then I can't see why John is so upset.

HELEN: I didn't tell him of Holt's visit. Not at the time. I didn't see why I should. How could I know that Nancy would begin talking and put me in the position of having to prove myself innocent? How could I know that even if the whole town talked, John would believe the story? It's so unlike him. He has a jealous streak, but I have never known him to take other people's words in preference to and discount mine.

GRACE: Then you have told him the truth? You've been able to talk? You gave me the impression that there was a wall between you.

HELEN: There is.

GRACE: Isn't there someone in town who can attest to the truth of your statement as to the exact date when Holt passed through? Did he stay at the hotel overnight?

HELEN: I'd rather die. Imagine me put in the position of having to prove that I did not have an affair with a man I hardly know, that my husband is the father of my child.

GRACE: You are quite right. I'd feel the same way. I don't know how I'd feel if Tom went out of his mind. But you've got to sacrifice pride sometimes—put yourself in a false position to get out of a false light. John is in a state. You are in a state. You yourself and John himself are temporarily eclipsed. You can't treat him as if he were his reasonable self. He isn't. You must treat his state. Tom has taught me this. Whenever a man and his wife get into states, each secretly demands some very definite and often very silly thing from the other. This thing, whatever it may be, becomes the focus of the emotions, and all of their weight centers here. Find out what this thing is that John demands, fulfill it no matter how foolish or unreasonable or unworthy it seems, and you will thereby release John from his state. And then you and he can really meet and clear up everything.

HELEN: I wish it were that simple.

GRACE: It may not be. It may be very complicated—but I'm speaking from experience. Tom has done it to me. He has watched me work myself into a state. He's let it run on to a certain point, then he's done the thing I wanted—and we were reconciled at once.

HELEN: You love each other.

GRACE: Don't you and John?

HELEN: I'm not sure of anything anymore. We seemed to be drifting apart. Then John built this house and we were happy together for a while. Then Mother came to live with us and we drifted apart again. Then when we knew the baby was coming we were happy again. We've never been as far apart as we are now.

GRACE: Tom will talk with John. Tom believes it is up to the man.

HELEN: He doesn't blame the woman?

GRACE: He's the only man I've known who doesn't. He believes that the basic trouble between men and women is caused by man not being what he should be, not doing what he should do. He not only believes it, he lives it.

Pause, silence.

HELEN: John may not talk. He may not give Tom a chance. You know how he is—or perhaps you don't. He has a pride too. He doesn't want it to seem that he needs help. He won't ever go to a doctor. He feels it's shameful to be sick, to be weak, to need help. He won't want to put himself in that position with Tom. He won't talk. He won't let Tom talk. He'll smile and seem to agree with everything; inside himself he'll be rejecting it all. He is simply awful that way. He fools everybody. For a long time he fooled me and I didn't know what was wrong. We'd work something out. I'd be sure we agreed. A few days later it would come out. John would do something that let me see that he really felt just the opposite all the time. I suppose we all are queer and difficult, but I can't imagine anyone more so than John—and why? That's what puzzles me. He has everything I wanted—and something has gone wrong.

GRACE: What?

HELEN: That's what I ask myself. He's not doing anything. If the house needs repairs he'll fix it. He goes shopping. Sometimes he cooks—and you know, he cooks excellently. He works with the car. We never need to take it to a garage. He goes fishing. He plays tennis. He does anything and everything that makes no demands of him; but as for serious work—he doesn't paint, he doesn't write, he doesn't even like to read anymore. The first week Lillian Range was here I began to have hopes.

GRACE: She wrote us she had met you and liked you and John the best of all.

HELEN: We felt that way about her. Mother became one of her great admirers. John got interested in writing and talking. Then something went wrong. I've never known what. That's the way it happens with us these days. We start things, we stop them. We drop people or they drop us. What is it, Grace? Have you found it in New York? Everyone seems so petty, so edgy, so ready to take offense, so queer, so suspicious, so—I don't know what it is. Or is it simply that I am growing up, coming to see the world as it really is, as it was all along when I thought everything was fine and happy unless I got hurt. Now I feel life is cruel—oh. It makes even a mother, me, wonder if I have a right to bring a child into such a world. And what will I do if John leaves me? It can't go on like this. Something must happen.

Helen's mother, Mrs. Ogline, *has entered the room unheard. She is an angular woman between fifty and sixty whose will has increased as her body [has] decayed. Her face is puffy, but its natural expression is hard. Once upon a time she had a charming smile. Now, in her old age, she remembers this smile and its effect on people, and she tries to recapture it, to imitate it, thus hoping to mask her avid determination to impose her will on others. Well-groomed, formal, Eastern in manners, she is like a corpse who has somehow acquired an aura of life. She stands in the doorway, having overheard the last part of the conversation between* Grace *and* Helen. *Now she makes a sound in her throat so as to inform the younger women of her presence.*

HELEN: (*turning around and rising*) Mother! Come in. This is Grace Elliot.

Mrs. Ogline *comes over and joins them, necessarily taking one of* John's *chairs as there are no others in the room. Though she hates the chair because* John *made it, it is as if he had made it for her. She is the only one who fits in it without an added sense of strain.* Grace *takes an instant dislike to her, and, as she is not adept at hiding a feeling of this kind,* Mrs. Ogline *sees it and takes a quick dislike to her, though concealing it under the mask of her smile.*

MRS. OGLINE: Helen has spoken often of you. She is so happy that you and your husband have arrived. I hear you motored the entire way.

GRACE: I hate trains.

MRS. OGLINE: You hate them? Isn't hate a strong word?

GRACE: One has strong feelings sometimes.

HELEN: Mother, they've taken the cute house I've pointed out on the road just before you enter the canyon.

MRS. OGLINE: I remember. Would you call it cute? You see, Mrs. Elliot, I do not share my daughter's enthusiasm for adobe. The *Century Dictionary*—I believe it is the *Century*—defines adobe as a brick used by people of inferior civilization. I must confess that I agree with the dictionary.

GRACE: A desk definition inspired by Anglo-Saxon conceit. Our bricks are not better and are not as beautiful.

MRS. OGLINE: Mud has never appealed to me as beautiful. Of course you have been to Europe, Mrs. Elliot. Do you really believe that even the best house in Taos is as beautiful as an English country house or a French château?

HELEN: Mother, that's an unfair comparison. You never saw one of the old haciendas.

MRS. OGLINE: Neither did you, my dear. I believed you knew what you wanted. I was so relieved to see that you wanted to settle down at last. I do not regret that I gave you the money to build in Taos; but now that I have lived here I must confess that I would prefer you in the East.

HELEN: You didn't *give* the money, Mother. It was a loan to John.

MRS. OGLINE: We won't go into that again.

HELEN: Why do you insist that you gave it? You know very well that John gave you his note. He has every intention of paying it back.

MRS. OGLINE: Every intention and no means. What makes people who know they cannot do it—pretend to borrow and pretend that they are going to repay? Wouldn't it have been more honest and manly of John simply to ask me for the sum, without all that rigmarole about a note and interest and what a fine opportunity for investment he was offering me? Fine investment, indeed.

HELEN: It was in the bank and not earning anything.

MRS. OGLINE: It was in the bank for you, my dear. My *investments* are managed by competent men. As a gift to you, even for a house in Taos, I have no regrets about it, but I repeat that I do resent the dishonest way in which it was obtained.

HELEN: It wasn't dishonest.

MRS. OGLINE: It is a pity that John doesn't defend you as well.

Helen *writhes and crumples.* Grace *is most uncomfortable, torn between a conflict of impulses. She wants to sit on* Mrs. Ogline. *She wants to get from the house and its situation which, as she sees more and more of it, strikes her as awful. She pities and wants to help* Helen, *but as yet sees no way to.*

MRS. OGLINE: *(to* Grace*)* Family difficulties should be kept from the ears of a stranger. That I was frank to speak of them before you, my dear, means that you are not a stranger in this house.

HELEN: She might wish she was.

Pause, silence.

MRS. OGLINE: I suppose you are a Taos addict, Mrs. Elliot? You believe the Indians are remarkable? You believe the Mexicans are picturesque? You are in love with the country?

HELEN: Taos isn't a drug.

MRS. OGLINE: I'm not so sure. Everyone who stays here any length of time acts strangely, as if she were under the influence of a drug. How else to explain it that white people of good families see uncouth savages and believe them a superior race? Indianitis, Mexicanitis, Taositis—different names for the same affliction.*

HELEN: Then why do you stay here if you dislike it so much?

MRS. OGLINE: I have my interests. Mrs. Coleman is a cultured woman and it is a pleasure to be in her company. I like to take drives when the roads permit, though John is not the chauffeur that my Orville is. And you, my dear, might do well to remember that you have need of me. (*to* Grace) As your little daughter grows up you will realize that after she is of age there are but few times when she really needs her mother. On such rare occasions you would, I am sure, endure a place much worse than Taos for the sake of being at her side.

The sounds of cars coming to a stop outside. Voices are heard approaching the door. Helen *arises to see who it is.* Lillian Range, Bill Bryne, *and* Tom Elliot *enter.* Lillian *shakes hands with* Helen, *greets* Grace, *and then goes up to* Mrs. Ogline. *For some strange cause there is a good relation between* Lillian *and* Mrs. Ogline. Tom *goes to* Grace. Helen *introduces* Bryne *and* Tom *to her mother. Then the women take chairs, the men remain standing.*

ELLIOT: (*to* Grace) We just met at the door. Lillian has been trying to find us all morning. She wants to leave tomorrow, would like to leave today.

GRACE: Not today, Lillian.

LILLIAN: You can't? I hoped you could, but tomorrow will have to do.

GRACE: I'm afraid not. A girl from the pueblo is coming to us today. We must get the house running. I wouldn't know what to do with Betty.

HELEN: Bring her here. I'd love to have her. How long will you be gone? Is it to Santa Fe you are going?

ELLIOT: Taking Lillian.

GRACE: Thank you, Helen. But Betty has been moved around so much the last month that I think she had better settle down in one place for a while.

* Toomer also offers "disease" above "affliction."

(to Lillian) Tomorrow is the earliest for us. I don't want you to go at all, but if you feel you must today, perhaps we can find someone who is going down.

LILLIAN: Tomorrow will be all right.

MRS. OGLINE: (to Lillian) I see you feel as I do—the sooner you leave Taos the better.

ELLIOT: I ran into John on the plaza and wanted to bring him out.

MRS. OGLINE: Must he be invited to his own house?

ELLIOT: It seems he must. (to Helen) I want you and John to have dinner with us tonight.

HELEN: Did he say yes?

ELLIOT: He wouldn't say.

HELEN: I can't, Tom. I'm taking Mother to Martha Coleman's.

ELLIOT: Take her, and then come to us.

HELEN: I'm invited, too.

ELLIOT: Break the date.

MRS. OGLINE: Is that your usual advice?

ELLIOT: My unusual advice.

HELEN: I don't see how I can, Tom. There'd be no one to drive Mother home. She doesn't want to stay late.

ELLIOT: Let her call the house whenever she wants to leave. I'll go for her.

GRACE: We have no phone.

ELLIOT: So we haven't. I don't know how it is to be worked out, but, Helen, I want you and John at the house tonight. Arrange it how you will, come early, come late—but come.

BRYNE: (to Helen) I'll be glad to drive your mother.

MRS. OGLINE: Am I to be parceled about and driven by the cheapest bidder? I knew I was making a mistake when I left Orville in the East.

ELLIOT: What becomes of you isn't so very important. I am frank to say that I am selfishly thinking only of your daughter and her husband.

MRS. OGLINE: Her husband! Does he dare still call himself that?

ELLIOT: Her mother—do you dare still call yourself that?

MRS. OGLINE: (to Helen) Am I to be insulted in your house?

HELEN: *(springing to her feet, crying, wringing her hands)* Oh, stop it, Mother. Stop it, Tom, please. I can't stand anymore. I'll scream. I'll go mad.

She begins sobbing hysterically. Grace *and* Lillian *go to her.*

The door opens and John Woodward *stands there, half in, half out, taking in the scene.* Mrs. Ogline *sees him as he sees her. She rises to her feet and stalks from the room.* John *steps back and out and slams the door.* Elliot *gestures to* Bryne *to follow him as he goes after* John. Grace *and* Lillian *get* Helen *into a chair and try to comfort her as she continues sobbing.*

13

Four-thirty that same afternoon. The Elliot *sitting room.* Grace *and* Tom *are at either side of the table, smoking pensively. Presently* Tom *speaks.*

ELLIOT: And thus do human beings bind each other in torment, in the shadow of the sacred mountain—pitiable beings in a magnificent earth. The futility of it, the shame, the ignobility. Something is wrong with us as a species. We lack the essential rightness that animals have. If we ever had it we have lost it. Not yet have we attained the essential rightness of man. These spiders that I kill are more perfect as spiders than we are as human beings. The shame, the ignobility of it—yet perhaps not futile. It is an unpalatable thought, but perhaps the truth is that we must go through just this, each one his own school of situation, for a purpose which no one has yet fathomed unless it be that of development. I believe it is so. Without this conviction I would scorn all but those who live for pleasure and get it; but imagine my telling a man on the rack, imagine my telling a starving man that his spirit needs hunger, imagine my telling the destitute that privation is the condition of their development, imagine me telling John that his spirit will profit by his present situation. If only I *knew*. If I were in touch with the reality of life, its processes and purpose—beyond belief, beyond guessing. Until I know I can do nothing. Happy are the deluded. Active are the dogmatic. All of one piece are those who never question but what their ideas are the truth.

GRACE: What do you think will happen?

ELLIOT: The world of men will go on as it has gone on, assuming that the word is the reality, talking words to each other, fighting and dying for ideas, using fire but never knowing its nature or purpose—and it may be just as well. Knowledge of purpose might shatter us. Few of us would have the courage to live if we could see and realize it all. Thank God for the original blinders, thank life for the gentle [corrosions]* of experience which open our eyes little by little, seldom giving us more than we can take in and when it gets too much for us we have at hand our own-made opiates. Chemical opiates, psychological opiates—those that dull us for a while until the shutter, too wide open, has closed. It must be frightful to be wide awake—unless in being wide awake you are thereby superior to hazard and empowered to cope with a universe of terrors. Perhaps it is so. Perhaps there are two kinds of security—the blind security of illusion, the conscious security of full knowledge of law. And we who live in between—

GRACE: *(with gentle amusement)* I meant what do you think will happen with Helen and John?

ELLIOT: *(suddenly looking at her)* Helen and John? What will happen? I don't know. It's a fight between John and Mrs. Ogline, and I question as to who will win.

GRACE: Not between John and Helen?

ELLIOT: Not at all. Not directly. His protest against Helen is only because through her he is linked and tied to her mother. The violent protest is against the mother. Remove her from the scene and you'd find that John and Helen would reconcile their differences at once.

GRACE: But the story?

ELLIOT: John has fastened on it only because it gives him a weapon against the mother through the daughter. Clear the scene of Mrs. Ogline, and you'd find John would reject the story. He doesn't believe it any more than you or I do.

GRACE: Did he say so?

ELLIOT: Of course not. It's the only weapon he has and he's going to cling to it until he needs it no longer. When I met him on the plaza I took him for a drive, and though he was tight-lipped as hell and resented what he felt to be

* Word obscure.

my inquisitiveness, I got enough from him to let me see the real trouble. You must have seen it at the house.

GRACE: I saw that mother.

ELLIOT: Had I known I was going to run into a scene like that I wouldn't have felt I had to ask John anything.

GRACE: Weren't you somewhat violent with Mrs. Ogline? Not that I minded in the least. I wanted to say all that and more. But I'm thinking of what you've tried to teach me—seeing the entire situation and thinking in terms of it. I'm glad you gave it to that horrible old woman, but haven't you made it more difficult for Helen and John?

ELLIOT: I have—deliberately. There's nothing I can do with that situation except speed it up, intensify it until it bursts. There's nothing else anyone can do. You can't tone it down. You can't relieve it. Any real change is impossible as long as it is as locked as it is. They are three people caught. The trap must increase in its own terms until it springs itself—at which time, at least two of the people will be released to do something [on]* their own terms. That's the point at which you and I can do something constructive. What happened when you and Lillian were left with Helen?

GRACE: We managed to quiet her.

ELLIOT: For the time. Anything more?

GRACE: Nothing more. It wasn't easy to do that. Lillian was so drained that I thought she might break down. And now she insists on bringing Frank Milner to tea. Says she feels she must bring us together before she leaves. I told her to go home and go to bed. But you know Lillian.

ELLIOT: You could imagine what happened when I went after John. As I got out of the house he was turning his car on the road. I ran toward [him] and he damn near ran over me. I jumped in our car and gave chase.

GRACE: You didn't.

ELLIOT: Just what I did. I didn't want to catch him, but neither did I want him to land in some bar around town and get drunk and spill everything. So, crazy though it seems, I kept my car behind him so as he could see it through his mirror until he was well away from Taos. Believing I'm on the lookout for him, he's not likely to turn up in Taos until the events of the

* in

morning have calmed down. That's the reason of it. I may add that I myself had some steam to let off, and I was feeling crazy enough to leap at the first means presented. I was in the car and after him—like that.

GRACE: In what direction did he go?

ELLIOT: Toward Questa.

GRACE: *(laughing at last)* I can just see the two of you—and clouds of dust behind the cars.

ELLIOT: A night in the mountains might cool him off.

Both have a laugh. Then—pause.

GRACE: I keep seeing that awful woman. How I'd hate to have to receive anything from her. Do you think that Helen and John are entirely dependent upon her?

ELLIOT: It may be. We've never known where their money came from.

GRACE: The thing that [started]* Helen this morning was when her mother mentioned the fact that she had given them the money to build the house. Imagine saying that before me. Mrs. Ogline insists it was a gift—with what strings attached we don't have to guess. Helen insists it was a loan. She says John gave his note for it. I was thinking—

ELLIOT: What?

GRACE: I was wondering if it would help any if we offered to advance them the money so's they could repay the mother. Could they get rid of her then? When I was there I wanted to push her. Not do it politely, not drag her—but just push her. I wanted to use my arms from the shoulder. I could have pushed her out of the house, pushed her out of Taos, just pushed her until my arms ached and were satisfied.

ELLIOT: I'm afraid not. Not yet. They've got to work something out before the money would do them any good. If they repaid her now they wouldn't be able to reject her. If we gave them money to go off on a trip, Helen wouldn't leave her, or they'd return to find her still entrenched, or if right now they went away and stayed away from her forever, there'd remain in John the very weakness that this situation is giving him [the] opportunity to

* stared

overcome. His pod is here. When and as soon as he has almost outgrown it, then will be the time when we can really help—help financially, morally, help in every way. Money given now would be effort wasted. The idea is good. Something of the same kind occurred to me. But, no. It wouldn't work. Not now. We'll keep it for later.

Pause, silence.

GRACE: What's the time?

ELLIOT: A few minutes after five.

GRACE: (*rising*) I must get the tea ready.

ELLIOT: (*also rising*) I must get ready to give Frank Milner what he doubtless deserves.

GRACE: (*going out*) Lillian's endurance is remarkable, everything considered, but I'm afraid she's overdoing this time. The best I could do was warn her.

Elliot *gets the bottle and the little glasses. As he puts them on the table there is a knock at the door. He goes and opens it.*

ELLIOT: Well, well. If it isn't good old Vin. How are you? Come in.

Vin. I've just a minute.

Vincent Weir *is of slight build and sensitive features. In personality he is pleasantly vague; in character he is quite firm, if anything he is overfirm in a determination not to let his good nature put him entirely at the service of others. Quiet-spoken and humorous, he is a lonely man, not young, not old, whom all people like, whom many admire because they feel he manages his life exceptionally well. He is a general favorite. One of his most unusual characteristics is that he minds his own business and minds yours only if you ask it of him. Editor of the local newspaper, asked around a great deal, knowing most of what is going on and being said, he gives the impression of never knowing anything.*

ELLIOT: Lillian Range and Frank Milner are coming for tea. Stay, won't you? I stopped by the office to ask you, but you weren't in. Grace and I wanted to see you.

VIN: Sorry, Tom. I've a date, I'm late now. I just wanted to tell you that I've found the owner of that property at last.

ELLIOT: No! The owner of our piece of land.

VIN: I have. He wants to sell. He says he's coming up to see you.

ELLIOT: How much?

VIN: A thousand dollars.

ELLIOT: Not bad. *(calling)* Grace, we've a visitor. Come quick. The press is here. The *Valley News* itself.* It has good news for us.

GRACE: *(coming in)* What's all the excitement? Hello Vin. Awfully glad to see you. What's it all about?

ELLIOT: Vin at last has isolated the elusive owner of our land.

GRACE: That is good news. Tell us about it.

VIN: There's not much to tell. A man named Fergusson says he is the owner and he wants to sell for a thousand dollars. It's a hundred and twenty acres. He'll be up to see you.

Grace *and* Tom *look at each other, still somewhat incredulous but delighted.*

VIN: I've wanted to come out to see you before but I've been rushed. You know how it is.

ELLIOT: We can well understand the demands made upon the editor of the successor to the first newspaper in New Mexico.

GRACE: You are staying for tea.

VIN: Sorry, I can't. I just ran out. I ought to be at another place now. *(going to the door)* I'm awfully glad you're back. I hope you do get that land.

ELLIOT: Thanks. If we do get it, it will be due entirely to your detective work. We'll build a house on it for you—how's that? It will be known as the Casa de Weir, or the Casa de Vin—whichever you prefer. We'll have two house warmings at once.

VIN: *(smiling)* Goodbye. I'll see you soon. Oh, shall I send the paper to you here?

* The *Taos Valley News* was a New Mexico newspaper from 1922–1936.

ELLIOT: Of course. We'd be lost without it. What's our box number, Grace?

GRACE: One three five.

Vin *makes a note of it, says goodbye again and goes out.*

ELLIOT: So something is actually moving at last.

GRACE: I'm glad. I had begun to feel that nothing would happen. I haven't told you, but I had a queer baffled feeling about it. I don't know why I should have. There are other fine spots. But we had set our hearts on this one, and when we couldn't even find out who owned it, and time passed—it's been nearly a year now—I felt baffled and suspended, almost as if we couldn't do anything else until we had decided on this, one way or the other. [I]* suppose I'm foolish. Why should just those hundred and twenty acres and a few trees on a mesa mean so much to me?

Tom *goes up to her and takes her in his arms.*

GRACE: Do you think I'm silly?

ELLIOT: I do not. What could be more real and natural? We want our own base out here. You, woman, want a place of your own choice and making. I, man, want my building. Together we want the land of our world—and we will have it.

He kisses her tenderly and they separate.

ELLIOT: This house isn't ours and it never will or could be. It doesn't belong to us. It's nice enough but not ours. It isn't that we don't own it, it is that we didn't make it. Both of us have the need to build our own.

GRACE: *(looking around)* We could improve it, though. None of our things are out. We've hardly unpacked. We've been living in our suitcases as if we were still on a trip. Tomorrow morning we must get settled.

ELLIOT: How's Peggy going to work out?

* I'm

GRACE: Very well, I think. She's eager and quick to learn. She's pleasant to have about. She's splendid with Betty. Most of the Indians have a way with children. There ought to be more time, but I suppose we can trust Betty with her tomorrow.

ELLIOT: Peggy—I can't link that name with an Indian girl. Wonder what her real name is.

GRACE: They seldom tell you. Isn't it getting late? Lillian is usually so prompt.

ELLIOT: It is. Maybe she has taken sick. By the way, did I tell you I ran into Martha Coleman on the plaza?

GRACE: No, did you?

ELLIOT: We stopped and slapped each other like a couple of children. She had [Hanna Gow]* with her. Mrs. Ogline is going there tonight. Quite a line-up the lady has. Upon a hill, a wreath of amazons—cactus to all men. *(he turns to the window)* Sacred mountain, Man-whalina, the new men have betrayed you, raped your earth, and ignored your spirit—and see the penalty; we are reversed upon the dust, while those who should be our women dwell like desert plants upon unwanted hills.

GRACE: Someone is coming.

She goes to the door and opens it to Lillian *and* Frank Milner.

* Lucy Frisk

APPENDIX A

Holograph Version of Scene 4

Enter: Hanna. The Landladies *pause to greet her but again set to work sweeping* the mud *dropping as the men on the roof continue their already monotonous pounding.*

Her rather handsome face is finely molded, suggesting that as a child she was delicate. She still is a high-strung, sensitive woman, semi-successfully concealed behind a mannish exterior. Pallid, she seems to powder, does use red lipstick. Though she rides horseback in the blazing sun she is curiously sunless, untanned—a chronic pale face. Her outfit is a pair of cowboy boots, blue jeans, blue shirt, and a five-gallon hat which she now swings in her hand.

HANNA: Hello. What's the upset? The roof not finished yet?

FIRST LANDLADY: Not yet. They promised to be done today, but you know how it is . . .

HANNA: Then why don't you wait? What's the use of trying to clean up?

Both Landladies *stop in their tracks, jolted by the sense of the question, yet unable and unwilling to admit that they have been engaged in needless, foolish work.*

FIRST LANDLADY: The Elliots are due.

HANNA: Let them come. They can be glad they weren't here when we all got washed out. A little dirt won't hurt them.

SECOND LANDLADY: That's what I said. Edith is—

FIRST LANDLADY: I am not, ~~Evelyn~~. How would you like to find your place unready after coming all the way from New York? I don't want them to have to stay at the Inn tonight.

HANNA: Why not? You aren't to blame. You didn't make it rain. You aren't the Mexican workmen. Don't take so much on yourself. A night at the Inn—what's that? They have money. Let them spend it and don't break your back. I don't like her.

SECOND LANDLADY: I know you don't. Why?

HANNA: The way she dresses—ugh.

SECOND LANDLADY: Nothing wrong that I can see, except that she does wear dresses.

HANNA: What do you mean?

SECOND LANDLADY: We may resent her because she's still feminine.

Hanna *and the* First Landlady *give the* Second Landlady *a most severe frown.*

HANNA: And I don't like him. He's all right, but he thinks he's god's own man, one of those real men who tame shrews and all that. I heard him talk last year. He carried on and kidded, but he was as serious as hell underneath. I smell that kind of fellow as you smell goats. I don't wish them any bad luck but I hope they both get drowned in the floods. Which way are they coming?

FIRST LANDLADY: Kansas is closed.

SECOND LANDLADY: Colorado isn't much better.

HANNA: Let's hope. Who wants them in Taos?

Both Landladies. We do.

HANNA: Of course. I'd welcome Jesus Christ if he'd rent my house.

A car is heard to stop on the road before the house. It starts again, and seems to be going around to the garage.

Both Landladies. (*with a start*) Could that be them?

HANNA: (*making a face*) We'll soon see.

Exit Landladies, *in a flurry.* Hanna *remains standing in the room, pensive, protesting, again swinging her black hat, uncomfortable that she has been caught in the situation of the* Elliots' *arrival.*

Outside there are hellos, greetings, a babble of voices.

Enter Landladies *with the* Elliots.

Tom Elliot *is a tall man of forty, shoulders somewhat stooped. He walks as if his body were stiff from driving. Dressed in gray flannel trousers, Norfolk coat. His first act is to take a critical glance at the room, appraising it, testing to discover if he is going to like living in it. He smiles to and greets* Hanna *by name, then sort of fastens on the ceiling, notices the particles of mud falling, hears the men pounding.*

Hanna *is abrupt but civil.*

Grace Elliot, *several years younger than her husband, enters as if her body, released from the car, were glad to be free to move around. Dressed in a gray sport suit tailored by Mrs. Franklin, Inc., New York. Happy to have arrived, she accepts the house, accepts the room, accepts the mud, the men pounding, and* Hanna, *even though she knows that they are not supposed to like each other.*

Each one talks, and the babble heard outside is now heard inside.

FIRST LANDLADY: So sorry we aren't ready for you.

SECOND LANDLADY: Have a good trip? How long did it take? How did you get through?

ELLIOT: Had to keep west and north to Cheyenne, and then down.

GRACE: I've read about floods but never seen them before.

ELLIOT: It was marvelous coming over Raton Pass this morning. What a day this was, a perfect day to enter the great Southwest.

FIRST LANDLADY: We expected to have everything done. The house was frightful. As I wrote you, the roof leaked and mud was everywhere. Some of your rugs and pillows are still in Santa Fe being cleaned.

GRACE: We can make out for tonight.

FIRST LANDLADY: Mary, did you get the laundry?

SECOND LANDLADY: Haven't had time.

GRACE: Is it ready? Can we get it?

FIRST LANDLADY: (*looking toward the ceiling*) Will those men never finish? I'm so sorry. You see, we couldn't clean up.

GRACE: Don't bother. We'll make out. You can imagine, we're anxious to unpack and get settled.

SECOND LANDLADY: Where is your little girl?

GRACE: She'll be in. She can take care of herself. She stays away from new people at first.

FIRST LANDLADY: *(again at the ceiling)* Now they're going over the other room. I'll just clean this up and then we won't track it through. *(she starts sweeping up)*

GRACE: *(to* Elliot*)* Let's unpack, shall we?

ELLIOT: Righto.

HANNA: I must go.

ELLIOT: Stay and have a drink with us. *(pulls out his watch)* Five-thirty. Half an hour past deserving time. We deserve a little something after our trip. Might as well begin to warm the house at once.

HANNA: No thanks. *(she moves toward the door)*

All move toward the door.

GRACE: *(to* First Landlady*)* Can I help?

FIRST LANDLADY: Someone had better get the laundry before they close.

Exit all. The sounds of women's voices come from the other rooms. Elliot *lugs in the bags and suitcases, quite a number of them. Each time he enters, he casts a fresh critical glance at the room. Finally he is finished, and sits down in a stiff leather Mexican armchair. While moving about he seems youngish, even boyish. Now, at rest and reflective, he takes on age.*

• • •

[. . .] them.

Now at last the Landladies *allow themselves to be seduced. They and* Grace *group around the table.* Elliot *pours drinks. The* Second Landlady *enjoys hers. The* First Landlady, *however, drinks absently, is still preoccupied with the house.*

FIRST LANDLADY: Those four chairs are rather nice, don't you think? Bought them in a drug store in Santa Fe. They are not very strong. If you need to stand on a chair, you'll use the hard wooden one in the kitchen, won't you?

ELLIOT: Certainly.

FIRST LANDLADY: Now about your bed. You wrote you want a double bed. Do you think that will do?

Elliot *arises, measures the bed with eyes, shakes his head.*

ELLIOT: I doubt it. We'll try it tonight and see. It's a three-quarters, isn't it?

FIRST LANDLADY: Mrs. Metchnecov has a large double mattress and spring which she said she'd be glad to lend.

ELLIOT: That's nice of her. (*to* Grace) Can't beds be bought in Taos?

Grace *and* First Landlady *exchange doubtful glances.*

ELLIOT: (*to* John) What about it, John? You have beds in your house, haven't you?

JOHN: (smiling) We have. We made the stands ourselves.

ELLIOT: And the springs and mattresses?

JOHN: Seems to me Helen got them in Santa Fe.

ELLIOT: Santa Fe seems to be the only source of supplies.

FIRST LANDLADY: Once a week a man will come to irrigate.

ELLIOT: We have a ditch on the place?

FIRST LANDLADY: Indeed. We have planted a garden.

ELLIOT: A garden? Really? Vegetable?

FIRST LANDLADY: We've planted radishes and onions and cucumbers—

ELLIOT: Excellent.

FIRST LANDLADY: Oh, Mr. Elliot. I wonder if you'd water the geraniums every morning and evening for the next several days. We put them in day before yesterday and there's been no rain.

ELLIOT: Glad to.

FIRST LANDLADY: (*rising*) You'll find them by the gate of the front fence, and just in front of the house. Before we go, are you sure there is nothing else you want?

ELLIOT: Nothing that I know of.

GRACE: We'll let you know if there is.

The Second Landlady *arises reluctantly, as if loathe to leave the bottle.*

SECOND LANDLADY: (*to* Elliot) Thanks for the drink. You don't often get that kind of stuff around here.

ELLIOT: Direct from New York, glad you liked it. Another nip before you go?

SECOND LANDLADY: I'd like to, but we must be off.

FIRST LANDLADY: (*moving to the door, looking toward the ceiling*) Apparently the men have stopped for the day. I don't think they'll need be over this roof again. Tomorrow they'll work over the kitchen and the other room. I'm so sorry, but we'll be around to help you clean up. By the way, you'll be wanting a girl, won't you? Mrs. Marcaranos, the woman who was helping me, would be glad to have the job. She's a good worker but can't speak a word of English. I'd be careful of the young girls. Some are good, some aren't reliable. If I can be of any help, please let me know.

GRACE: We will.

FIRST LANDLADY: Goodnight—and we hope you'll find everything and have a good first night.

SECOND LANDLADY: Goodnight.

The Landladies *are seen to the door and waved off.* Elliot *stays out.* Grace *and* John *return to the room, settle around the table, light cigarettes.*

GRACE: Tell me about Lillian. Is she still here?

JOHN: So far as I know. I saw her the other day on the plaza and she said she was going to stay until you and Tom came.

GRACE: What's the matter?

JOHN: Says she must go to Santa Fe to be examined.

GRACE: Is that really it?

JOHN: Don't know. She's had a pretty hectic time. I'm afraid she hasn't been happy here. She looks ever so much better. You can see the improvement in her physical shape. When she arrived she was very tired, quite sick. From New York to Taos for one in her condition is no joke. Now she looks much better and says she feels it. But something is going on. She's caught up in something.

GRACE: Something? What? People?

JOHN: What else? You know how people are here.

GRACE: No, I really don't. I've heard, but I've never experienced it. I've always lived off, as you know.

JOHN: It's true. Take them by themselves, each one separately, and you won't find finer people anywhere. But together—and they're always together because they are few and the country is so vast—I can't begin to tell you all the ins and outs, rivalries, jealousies, back biting—I keep out, as much as I can. Lillian was in it before I could warn her.

GRACE: She has always attracted people.

JOHN: So she has.

GRACE: In New York she literally had to bar her doors and keep her phone number a secret except to a few.

JOHN: She's in a horrible little place. Pink walls, no view, an iron bed. Any time you go there you'll find people coming in. She's helpless. They see her from the window. There's only one door.

GRACE: Awful. We feel responsible. It was because of all we said about Taos and the Southwest that she came out here.

Enter Elliot.

ELLIOT: We are going to have a problem with that young lady of ours. She's a sociable young lady, John. If there are children anywhere about she'll find them. I just found her trying to cross the road and take up with a gang of kids across the way. The cars come down this dusty highway at fifty and more—and more dust than I want. She can't judge the speed. She's had no experience of cars. What's more, she won't see them coming. We've got to stop that.

GRACE: *(on her feet)* Where is she?

ELLIOT: In the yard now—for how long I don't know. The gate was closed, but she found the cattle guard. I've instructed her, but I'm damned if I see how we are going to keep her in. Nor do we want to. She's got to have children to play with. We can't police her all the time, what's the answer?

All are thoughtful. Grace *resumes her seat.* Tom *takes a chair.*

ELLIOT: What about the Mexicans, John? Had any experience with Mexican kids?

JOHN: As far as I know they're all right, just like any other kids. Be able to tell you better in several years.

GRACE AND ELLIOT: Is Helen—someone wrote us.

JOHN: (*with lowered head, nods*) Due any time after the tenth.

GRACE: I'm glad for Helen. She has wanted one, hasn't she? Tom, we must go out to see her.

JOHN: (*rising*) So must I. I've been away too long as it is.

ELLIOT: Any good doctors in Taos?

JOHN: It depends. She'll be taken care of, all right. As you can see by looking around, quite a few children have been delivered into the world in New Mexico. No New York specialists—but, somehow or other, the larger part of the human race seems able to get along without them.

ELLIOT: (*to* Grace, *as they move toward the door*) What are we going to do about dinner tonight? We have nothing here. Go to the Tavern?

JOHN: Wish I could ask you but I'm cook now and we weren't sure when you'd turn up.

ELLIOT: To the Tavern for us. John, suppose you and Helen join us. Come on, we'll all go in and get her.

~~*Exit. Curtain.*~~

GRACE: And Lillian too.

~~*Exit. Curtain.*~~

ELLIOT: Our first dinner in Taos in the great Southwest.

Exit. Curtain.

APPENDIX B

Fragments from the Holograph

[. . .] some wooded with enormous pines, some bald and baked

Though the mountains do not move, you move. You wind around and up and down huge masses, going over a pass of some 9,000 feet and sweeping down, perhaps through a shaded canyon, to a mere 6,000 feet of open plateau country, treeless, far-stretching, desert-like in its intensity. Storms come and go; and if you are driving an open car you may be burnt by the sun in Taos but drenched before you get out of the canyon on the road to Santa Fe.

Certainly we cannot take it casually, we who belong here yet have no place of our own.

• • •

ELLIOT: Who can? They are always the questionable factor. The earth, yes. Trees and stones, even water in a dry country. Night and day, the sun and stars. But human beings? I know that this is great earth. At this time of reckoning, however, I have our strong affirmation and two interrogations. In order that we accurately understand each other, I think, John, I had best give you an abstract of my views on these matters—clear if not profound views, as you will see.

JOHN: By all means.

ELLIOT: As regards a locale, there are three large matters to be considered. First there is the physical element, the obvious physical geography of the place. Physical New Mexico is magnificent. I know of no place in the world so magnificent and at the same time inhabitable. The Rio Grande Valley is one of Nature's great dramas. It is quite wonderful that the human species can also inhabit it and enact its kind of drama amid such play of elements and natural splendor. I have nothing but affirmation for physical New Mexico in general and the Taos region in particular.

JOHN: Agreed.

ELLIOT: Second there is the human element, the people themselves, the obvious living conditions, the subtle human atmosphere of the place. As I say, I have a question mark behind these items.

JOHN: Agreed.

ELLIOT: Third, there is what we may call the supernatural element, the superphysical, the extrahuman. Stout realist that you claim to be, you must admit that everywhere, especially here in Taos, there is something beyond facts and things, beyond reason and the rational. This is the soul of the place, a compound of the overtones of the geographical and the human elements. Or, for all I know to the contrary, there may enter in elements pure and simple supernatural. Most superstitions are plain delusions. But some superstitions, I firmly believe, are nothing more or less than our imperfect recordings of that in life that transcends our one brain. I could easily become superstitious in Taos. The minute I get here I feel something uncomfortable opening up in the nether regions of my emotions. The opening becomes wide at night. Night in Taos puts a gap in me that goes straight through civilization and education to the primitive core—we'll call it that. Naturally I ~~fight it~~ struggle against it. ~~This fight throws me into conflict.~~ I'm not sure if the soul of Taos is friendly or inimical to me. And so, while affirming physical New Mexico, while questioning the human factor, I fight against a certain dread, a fear, a terror almost, feeling that when I come to this place I come to my doom. Ever have such feelings?

JOHN: No, can't say that I have.

• • •

JOHN: Then dig in here. This is great earth. The human beings I can't guarantee.

ELLIOT: Who can? I know it is great earth. But what should be simple is strangely complicated. Doubtless I overcomplicate it. Millions of people have found or accepted their environment without all the fuss I'm making.

JOHN: Can't have everything. Choice of one thing means loss of another. You've got to decide what you want most.

ELLIOT: I realize it. No, not everything. (smiles) Perhaps it is like this. Grace and I are happy together. Having no problems between ourselves, we go out of our way to make problems with our surroundings. There must be difficulty, you know. We've got to struggle with and overcome something.

JOHN: Settle here, and you'll have troubles enough.

ELLIOT: I'm sure of it. I do Grace an injustice, though. She's quite ready to buy. I'm the one who holds back. I held back last year—and so, this summer, we are committed to this little two by four adobe abode. We would be in our own place, if it weren't for me. I'll hold back this year.

JOHN: Why?

ELLIOT: Don't quite know. Wish I did. There's something. It may be in me. It may be out there in the country. Whatever it is, it is strong.

JOHN: But here you are.

ELLIOT: That's the strange part of it. We'd come through force, I am sure, if it were necessary. I can't stay away. The Southwest reaches all the way to New York. This time we came through floods to reach here. On the other hand, after a while, the Southwest repels me back to New York. Isn't that a crazy way to be?

JOHN: It surely is.

ELLIOT: Though it may and I surely hope it will be different this time. Meanwhile, the years are passing—and not yet have I my establishment. It's ridiculous—because, as they say, we have the means. Like the earth itself, like human society everywhere, I become increasingly restless. Perhaps the truth is that there will be no rest for the weary until all the weary are at rest.

APPENDIX C

Toomer's Notes

Also for *Drama of the Southwest**
Ma-guōlena
Ma-whōlena
Ma-chuōlena

Notes

The slope of Machuōlena.† A symbol of the slope. All automatic society is running down, breaking up, struggling to form new automatic societies, possibility of the creation of a conscious society.

The great question of life—if human existence is for the purpose that human beings may develop souls, if struggle is the basic condition by means of which souls are developed, then all difficulties and all struggles are valuable, and this age in which nothing runs smoothly is the age of great opportunity. If however man in only his body, then struggle is at the best no more than a natural necessity which must be met by man for no advantage, and this age is the age of great mistakes.

The background—that of the mountain at night—symbolizes: the beginning, the source to which all things return at the end. It is being, it is eternity, it is silence. The foreground, that of day and human activity symbolizes: human development, struggle, restlessness. In the first third of the play

* This line, and the macrons, are added in pencil. The remainder of the notes are typed.

† Toomer seems to be trying various out transliterations for the name of Taos Mountain. Tom Elliot uses "Mawhaulina" in scene 9 and "Man-whalina" in scene 13.

increase restlessness to a climax, have people come and go. In the second third of the play have it move so that the foreground and the background blend. In the third third of the play, there is again restlessness, but now the restlessness is of the nature of divine discontent.

A quotation of an ancient saint, "Happy is he who has no soul. Happy is he who has a soul completely formed. But suffering is the lot of whoever has a soul in the making."*

When people are harassed, are hard-pressed, they protest. In such a condition, the primary protest is that of cruelty, the desire to punish. Brutality is the order of the day. If the protest is or seems futile, then cruelty is unmitigated. But when and as the protest makes its way towards fulfillment, then tenderness alternates with brutality and tempers it, and when a new era dawns, tenderness blends with cruelty to produce a new affirming strength. In the old peoples of New Mexico, those whose civilization has not yet been broken up, namely in the Indians and the Mexicans there still exists a certain blending of tenderness and cruelty. In the white people of New Mexico, they whose civilization is breaking up, they who feel the impingement of world chaos—in the worst of them there is brutality and debauchery, in the best of them tenderness alternates with cruelty (they are friendly today, nasty tomorrow) and not as yet have tenderness and cruelty blended into a new stable and assured strength. This will be shown in certain of the characters that revolve around the Elliotts.† The Elliotts themselves, having left their world, being in the process of establishing themselves in this new place are without atmosphere at first, and hence exposed to the currents and crosscurrents of Taos. Their harmony will be disorganized, and they will epitomize what is happening to people everywhere. They will feel the primary emotions of human life when put in a nude situation. Fear, anger and rage, cruelty—until, by spiritual alchemy, these emotions are tempered and blended in the process of humanization.

The meaning of the Elliots' search for land and a place of establishment: this symbolizes the attempt of human values to materialize and have their place in the life of the contemporary world. That they do not fully succeed in

* A version of this proverb was painted on the canopy of the study house at Gurdjieff's institute at Fontainebleau, France. In a 1929 article on the institute, Carl Zigrosser reported it as reading, "Happy is he who has no soul; happy is he who has a soul; terrible is it for him who has a soul germinating in him." Toomer puts the proverb in Tom's mouth in scene 4.

† This spelling of Elliot occurs twice here and nowhere else in the drafts.

the outside world, means the time is not yet, that other issues and values must be the chief interests of man for yet awhile. An oasis is needed, perhaps an ark; but these two are increasingly difficult to obtain.

Between a person and his environment a balance must be maintained—an equalization of tension. If the environment completely and continually invades the person, the person goes insane—as has actually happened to a solitary man adrift on the ocean for days—as happens even more frequently with shepherds. If the person overmasters the environment to an extreme degree, he too goes insane, insane with egotism. In so-called normal life a balance is maintained—at one time the environment may overmaster him, at the next he may overmaster it—but there is an exchange, a fluctuation, and, over a long period, it can be seen that the person and his environment are more or less evenly matched. Periods of new experience and creation, however, are often proceeded by a period in which a person is almost obliterated by the outside world. The ecstasy of creation is preceded by the ecstasy of annihilation.

• • •

Taos is an end product. It is the end of the slope. It is an end product of the Indians, an end product of the Spaniards, an end product of the Yankees and puritans. It must be plowed under. Out of the fertility which death makes in the soil, a new people with a new form may grow. I dedicate myself to the swift death of the old, to the whole birth of the new. In whatever place I start work, I will call that place Taos. (taken from *Drama of the Southwest*)*

* The folder of Toomer's notes contains three copies of this paragraph: a handwritten version and a typed copy and its carbon. Though each copy carries the assertion that the paragraph is "taken from *Drama of the Southwest*," no surviving portion of the manuscript contains it.

APPENDIX D

Letters from 1934

A Note on the Letters

These letters and telegrams passed between Jean Toomer and Marjorie Content in June of 1934, as she was traveling to New Mexico with Georgia O'Keeffe. It was a crucial time for Toomer and Content. The two had finally been introduced in spring of 1934 by Fred Leighton, one of their many mutual acquaintances and friends.* Romance blossomed quickly. Content was separated from her third husband at the time, and in the letters she and Toomer alluded to her plans to consult a lawyer about "business"—a divorce—as soon as she reached New Mexico. Toomer joined her there in July and the pair married on September 1, one day after her divorce was finalized. O'Keeffe stood as witness.

Content's bright descriptive style is one of the great, revelatory pleasures of this exchange of letters, giving remarkable insight into the ways she experienced the landscapes she passed through with O'Keeffe. One evening in Colorado, O'Keeffe suggested Content take a photograph of a wheat field and Content promised to name the resultant photograph "Portrait of Georgia O'Keeffe." Both laughed at the idea, but in their exultant freedom, these "world riders" created impressions of themselves on the land through acts of perception and image making. To move through and see the Western landscapes was to draw themselves.

* Fred Leighton was active in Gurdjieff groups in Chicago and New York. First in Chicago and later also in New York, Leighton operated an Indian Trading Post that sold Mexican, Navajo, and Pueblo handicrafts, and he helped nurture the market for these goods with elaborate public lectures and displays of Indian artifacts throughout the Chicago area.

I have endeavored to preserve the stylistic idiosyncrasies in Content's beautiful handwritten letters, including her frequent use of long dashes and tendency not to capitalize after some periods. Her punctuation conveys enthusiasm for life to the point of nearly breathless excitement for the journey underway, the new beginning ahead with Toomer, and for her recent successful introduction to Toomer's midwestern circle. This circle included friends from his days as a teacher and leader of Gurdjieff groups in Chicago and Wisconsin—groups dedicated to using the mystic G. I. Gurdjieff's methods to reach higher consciousness—as well as the family of Margery Latimer, Toomer's first wife. With the exception of his letters of June 7 and July 1, Toomer's letters are typed. They nonetheless preserve a sense of intimacy with a looseness of style and profusion of affectionate language.

The mood of epistolary honeymoon that pervades the journey is spoiled when Toomer becomes frightened by Content's failure to send a telegram upon reaching New Mexico. His vulnerability would be touching (a slip of paper preserves a telegram he composed: "Wires have been hot to locate you . . . you mustn't disappear like that") save that he is angered by her dereliction and plays the bully and the boor, typing off several hurtful letters.* In this impassioned and sometimes stormy final parting before their marriage, Toomer and Content articulate their relationship to each other and to the Southwest.

The letters also clearly convey Content's solicitude for O'Keeffe's physical well-being and the state of her spirits during the journey. She had played nurse to O'Keeffe before, most significantly in the spring of 1933, when they traveled together to Bermuda while O'Keeffe was recovering from a nervous breakdown or debilitating depression.† After more than a year without painting, O'Keeffe resumed painting in January of 1934 around the time of Toomer's winter visit to her at Lake George as companion or lover.‡ She went to Bermuda again that spring, this time alone, and blessed the sudden relationship between Toomer and Content that sprung up in her absence, but her health was still somewhat shaky when she and Content set out for New Mexico. This O'Keeffe at forty-six is far different from the indomitable and iconic

* These more claustrophobically personal letters of June 13, 14, and 19 (the latter composed in a new fit of anger when he receives her letter of June 16 explaining the unsent wire and finds its explanation insufficient) may be found in Box 8, folders 253–54.

† Robinson, *Georgia O'Keeffe*, 390.

‡ Ibid., 393–402.

southwestern septuagenarian, octogenarian, and nonagenarian she would become, scrambling up ladders and rowboating in canyons. Toomer's queries and Content's answers about O'Keeffe's health suggest the two saw themselves engaged in a precarious operation to convey a very precious and delicate cargo to New Mexico. Even the newly purchased car that Toomer planned to drive west for her was an invalid's accommodation: O'Keeffe purchased it because she feared she would not be strong enough to paint in the open air again and hoped to work from inside it.

Toomer and Content, both headstrong, creative people in their own right, are deferential to O'Keeffe, who, in letters to her husband, Alfred Stieglitz, praised Content for her quietness and attention during this time. Toomer and Content played a number of roles in the creative community that circulated between New Mexico, New York, and beyond, and these letters illuminate some of those roles. Like so many neonatives and visitors to New Mexico, Toomer and Content turn evangelical and seek to bring others to the Southwest after them. Thus Toomer attempts both a mentor's marital counseling and a booster's travel planning in the lives of his Gurdjieff disciples Chaunse Dupee and Tockie Green. Toomer's relationship to the pair may be mirrored in Tom Elliot's intervention in the Woodward marriage in *A Drama of the Southwest*. Though of lesser means and less full commitment to New Mexico than figures like Mabel Dodge Luhan and Mary Austin, Toomer and Content each play host and patron in the Southwest in smaller ways, contributing to their own happiness and their status in the art colony by attracting other artists and friends to the region. Thus shades of Martha Coleman, trailing summer houseguests across Taos Plaza like a comet, might be found in many a Taos resident.

The Toomer-Content letters also record encounters with other figures such as Fred Leighton and Ralph Hubbard, meetings that point to the ways in which Toomer and Content's circles overlapped considerably with networks of people involved in buying, selling, performing, and promoting Native American crafts and culture. Thus, on their way to Taos, where they will spend time with Pueblo friends and acquaintances (including Tony Lujan), Content and O'Keeffe pause with Ralph Hubbard, a famous Indian hobbyist and leader to a nationwide movement of those who would preserve Native American cultural practices they perceived to be endangered or vanishing by practicing them themselves. Hints at many of the figures we meet in *A Drama of the Southwest*—artists, Tough Girls, patrons, hosts, and Indian experts—are here in these letters.

• • •

Letters from 1934

Jean Toomer to Marjorie Content
Letter on stationery of Russell S. Walcott,* Barrington, IL
Thursday, June 7, 1934, 7:20 p.m.

My dear,

I want to say, "Oh yes, just because she was my sweet bunny." But my sweet kitten-cat is somewhere west in Illinois or even in Iowa by now. And she won't get this until she reaches Santa Fe.

I felt empty and sad as you drove away, as Eugenia and I returned to Barrington.†

Immediately upon arriving here, I had to do something; so I worked on my car (which is called the gascar) and Betsy and I took it for a road test.‡ It is o.k. Tomorrow I set sail for Milwaukee.

Eugenia remarked that you and Georgia should have been given a greater send-off.

Eugenia went over to Evanston to her father's for dinner.

Russell + Betsy and I had dinner here. Now Russell has gone off for a consultation with one of his clients—and I am keeping house by myself for a while. I am going to write these lines to you, and then go up and make myself handsome by shaving, etc.—which I did not have time to do before dinner.

* Russell Walcott was a modernist designer of homes in fashionable suburbs in northern Illinois and Wisconsin.

† Eugenia B. Walcott, wife of Russell Walcott, had been a friend and patron to Toomer since the 1920s. In 1929, she supported him financially with a monthly stipend. Around 1934–1935, Content was lending financial support to artists and writers. His impending union with Content would begin to place Toomer on the other side of the artist/patron relationship.

‡ Betsy is Betsy Ann Walcott, Russell and Eugenia Walcott's three-and-a-half-year-old daughter.

Russell wanted to send a telegram to you "Somewhere in Iowa" to greet "the Tough Girls" after they crossed the Mississippi. But we didn't know where to send it.

He says both he and Eugenia liked you very very much—and Eugenia says she had a great time with Georgia during the trip to Geneva. Russ is sorry he missed meeting Georgia.

Betsy calls you "The Lady with the Bracelets"—and when she saw me today she asked where "my girl" was. I said, "What girl?" She said, "Your girl. The girl who came here with you."

During dinner Russell + I talked of the Southwest. He wants Eugenia and himself + Betsy to go down there, and he said that now that Eugenia knew you and Georgia, it oughtn't be so difficult for her. He had the idea (which is true) that Eugenia ought to but won't leave here because she dreads the difficulties of new adjustments. Well, they just may come out.

I hear a train whistle off in the distance. It awakens my strange sadness and nostalgia. How it reminds me poignantly that you are physically away from me for the first time in—how long?

I feel it; yet I don't fully realize it yet. I worked on the car, and that helped—as driving the car helped you. Then I did things "went places" with Betsy. Then Russ came home and we had long drinks—not of Scotch but of bourbon.

And now I'm going to look over Russell's manuscript of his book—and I'm awaiting your wire. The first night of the S. S. Packard without the Admiral.

—— 10:45 p.m.

Your wire just arrived from Cedar Rapids—and we all were glad to hear.

—— June 8, 10:25 a.m.

I'm at the Barrington post office—off for Milwaukee—and you are going across Iowa—

love to "she was just a sweet one"

Jean

Marjorie Content to Jean Toomer
[Posted in Belle Plaine, IA, Friday, June 8, 1934]*
Thursday evening
1 Mile West of Cedar Rapids
9:30 p.m.
Central Standard Time

And so my first letter to you.

I didn't much like driving away from you there—but since then it hasn't been so bad—you have been sitting right there in Mr. Packard a good part of the time—And when you weren't there I could talk about you a bit—for of course I couldn't do <u>that</u> with you sitting right there.

Well my darling what do you think we did—right off the bat?

Started as you directed and at the very next corner, we turned left following US 30 signs, and after going a couple of miles I said to Georgia—These aren't the towns we should be going toward.

There we were heading back to Chicago!!—

So round about and duly started west expecting that we might bump into you + Eugenia in Geneva—but caught no glimpse.

Georgia says that Eugenia had a strange + shocked expression as she caught sight of us saying goodbye from the other side of the car. Perhaps you are having some questions to answer there tonight!

Georgia has been very good—wanting to go on + on—saying that she was not at all tired—enjoying the country and telling me tales of her parents and grandparents and early childhood.

There are <u>very</u> few places to eat and sleep in these parts and none of them very attractive—

Getting hungry about 7:15 we finally stopped in a small town (Lowden, Iowa) at the village cafe. It didn't look like much but we each had a good steak—and some sliced tomatoes and I had a three-masted schooner of beer, while G indulged in a sloop! (Nautical terms to be forgiven if inaccurate—I'll improve.)

I didn't look at the mileage tonight before retiring (yes—I'm in bed) but think we must have gone nearly 200 miles—1st stopped once for orange juice—2nd once to send you postcards announcing the transformation of two nice little girls from small eastern towns—4th once to send you a dozen telegrams—3rd once for dinner and then drove to (5th) here—an auto camp—where we expect to pass a good night—

* Later notations in Marjorie Content's hand provide postal information.

The country is quite nice—big farm lands—rather flat—rather unexciting but very pleasant—

Temperature neither hot nor cold—Stiff following wind—We ran before it at a steady 60 per on fine roads—

I'd better stop my dear—and let Georgia get to sleep—

Lights out—Heigh ho for Santa Fe and eventually you—

More Tomorrow—

——————

Hailed by Georgia at some time before 7 a.m. Georgia having been up stamping around while I slept on—saying that she waked up feeling very peppy + not at all tired. Just not at all. Find we went 206 miles yesterday—

Had a fine sleep + today the sun is bright. The wind abated—the top down. Breakfast about to be served—See you later.

M*

Marjorie Content to Jean Toomer
[Posted June 9, 1934]
Shelton, Neb.—
Friday, June 8, 1934†

Jean—my dear—would you believe it? Today we have come something like 420 miles—?

We didn't start very early—we stopped frequently—and yet here we are in bed and it's just 10 p.m.—

We have passed thru uncomfortably hot spots—sheets of rain—hail—cold—and then hot again—crossed rivers (Missouri and Platte) gone over hills—and flatlands. Georgia drove one stretch of 20 miles and another about 35—Says she feels fine—

I dipped into the flask for the first time before dinner this evening and even G. wet her tongue with it—You should have seen the cloudburst just after lunch—such sheets that you couldn't see anything. We crept on for miles until we saw some buildings and we stole into what proved to be a garage—The street in front was a river which went down somewhat before we left. The hail cracked fearsomely but damaged nothing. G. had them all excited because she began looking at Fords and with the possibility of a sale—They frothed with excitement.

† Content's dateline reads "Thurs.—" but is incorrect; this letter seems to have been written a full travel day after she stopped near Cedar Rapids on Thursday, June 7.

I've been wondering about you and won't hear for a few more days. How the Paige ran—where you stayed—what you have met with.

We have fared exceeding well. Strange-looking cafes supply surprisingly nice plain food—No more charming farmhouses such as you + I met with—no more chicken dinners—Beer + steak persist however—as do pleasant gas stations presided over by pleasant people—Everybody smiles more readily in these parts. The easy western way + the wave of the hand.

The country has been lovely—seems to be more rain here, except for one section which was quite toasted and thoroughly grilled—All through there the cows inhabited the side of the road—munching—looked after by farmers' children carrying red flags to warn drivers that cows are erratic creatures. Just before the storm the sky was so wonderful that it was difficult to watch the road. Great masses of grey transparencies overlaid darker grays. and the sun shot through in unexpected loopholes—

Saw three cows in your favorite position simultaneously and heard your laugh ring out beside me.

This camp's cabins have only one bed each, and so G. + I have separate cabins tonight—

But in spite of that I'm going to out the lights—for a good sleep will be welcome—

At dinner Georgia and I touched somewhat on "the cottage," Gurdjieff (?)—groups in general.

The lady is certainly afraid of them—the groups I mean. As for you she is a hearty endorser. She also thinks that you + I are particularly well suited to one another—That's an odd idea—isn't it?—

Goodnight—my darling—

M

———————

At 6:30 a.m.—Georgia + I walked out of our respective cabins at the same instant—both headed to the same place—She has gone back to catch a few more winks—But there is no attraction there for me—A clear sun is shining on a soaked and windswept earth—Breakfast calls!

This—I hope you noticed at the head of this letter is Shelton and I think it particularly appropriate for G. to be staying here.* Yesterday morning, I picked the name without imagining that we would get this far. and then, forgetting Shelton and its special fitness, we tried to stop at Grand Island—but didn't like the looks of the camping on the Wood River only two cabins and full up—and so it was written on the tablets that Shelton it must be—

* O'Keeffe and her husband, the photographer Alfred Stieglitz, shared a suite at the Shelton Hotel in New York from 1925–1936.

Since yesterday morning and the heat, I have been dressed in a dress of Georgia's which was easy to get at—green + white striped cotton—would go one + a half times around my waist—It's very comfortable as it doesn't touch my body in any spot—and the wind showers me even though it be a hot wind. Not hot this morning.

I want my coffee. If she isn't up I'm going downtown + have it + come back for her.

Au revoir—sweet

M*

Marjorie Content to Jean Toomer

Telegram from Limon, CO

Saturday, June 9, 1934, 7:00 p.m.

JEAN TOOMER

PORTAGE WIS

HUBBARDS RANCH† AT ELBERT TONIGHT AND TOMORROW ALL FINE

NOT SIGNED‡

Jean Toomer to Marjorie Content

Portage, WI

Sunday, June 10, 1934, 10:30 a.m.

Darling,

Your wire from Limon, Colo, just came. Bravo! What world-riders you are! I'm going to send you a wire c/o Hubbards Ranch, and I'd like to put in it, Holé, World-Riders! But I'm afraid the telegraph people might not quite understand the holé!§ Anyway, I'm going to wire, because ever since you left I've wanted to reach you somewhere in route with greetings, and because I can perhaps get a return wire from Georgia as to Russell driving her car west to Barrington.

Yes, it was a good thing that we both had something to do, after that parting at Geneva. I'm afraid I was rather a silent presence all the way back to Barrington. Then, as I wrote in my first letter, I immediately got to work putting Little Gascar in shape. I had to work.

But what! So you turned around in Geneva and were heading back for Chicago!!

† Content and O'Keeffe stay with Ralph Hubbard, the prominent Indian hobbyist and worldwide promoter of Indian dance and culture who wrote the book *American Indian Crafts* (1935).

§ This Spanish-language expression of praise or encouragement properly spelled *¡Olé!*, is roughly equivalent to *Bravo!* or *Well done!*

I'd have done the same thing. I like to feel that even the S. S. Packard didn't want to leave me.

And so! You and Georgia put your heads together about me! I mean, some of the time.

No, no questions to answer to either Eugenia or Russell that night. Betsy called you, my bracelet girl, and that seemed to be that. Russell was sorry he missed seeing Georgia. A good part of the evening we looked at maps, wished we could reach you with a wire; and we talked about the Southwest, Russell in private saying to me that Eugenia is very tired, and should go away for a while, but that she shrinks from having to make radical adjustments to strange places, but that, in this case, since she already knew you and Georgia, it ought to work out fine. He tried to persuade her. I did a bit. She finally said she might consent to go, provided that she be at liberty to return after a few days. I don't know. In any case, they know I'll leave around the first of July; and it just may be that they will too.

That evening, too, Russell read me sections of his book; and was much set up when I said it was going splendidly.

I'm awfully glad Georgia is responding to the trip so well. We felt she would, didn't we? And, I gather, no tire trouble as yet. I hope none.

And village cafes, and tourists camps!

Have you run into any storms? And, my oh my, no one less than Dillinger* is supposed to be in the Iowa region. Mother Latimer† suggested that perhaps you and Georgia, very tough girls by now, had captured him.

I drove the little car to Milwaukee without a falter, being surprised when it ran along merrily at a 40 mile an hour clip. But all manner and description of cars passed me, as if I were standing still. I still had only my old '33 plates, and as I drove down Milwaukee's main street, with cops at each corner, I expected to be stopped again and again. But no. I got through. I found Chaunse looking sort of haggard. We left for Portage that same afternoon, via Oconomowoc, where I again saw Yvonne, Mrs. Dupee, and Chaunse's son, Gordon.‡ Mrs. Dupee as well as Yvonne asked about you—and many times already I've told of the departure from Geneva.

* John Dillinger, notorious bank robber and gangster, had escaped from prison and was robbing banks in the Midwest around this time.

† Mother Latimer was Laura Latimer, the mother of Jean Toomer's first wife, Margery Latimer, with whom he was staying in Portage while putting Margery's letters in order for possible publication. Mother Latimer would remain close to Toomer and Content and her granddaughter, Margery "Argie" Toomer Latimer, all her life. Kerman and Eldridge, *Lives of Jean Toomer*, 222.

‡ Yvonne Dupee and her brother Charles (Chaunse or Chaunce) were friends from the Gurdjieff movement. Yvonne participated in the Portage experiment and supplied Toomer with funds for his summer in Fontainebleau in 1929 (Kerman and Eldridge 188).

Yesterday morning my '34 plates arrived. I put them on. Moreover, I bestirred my [old]* self and gave the car a good washing with the garden hose, and then, my goodness, did a first-rate polishing job! It took most of the morning, in the hot sun. But the little car responded. It really did. And I drove mother downtown for shopping, with the car shining—and several people not only hailed me but hailed the car, as if it were an old good friend. And mother—my, what that car means to her! She was as pleased with its return as if it were a child of the family. To everyone she sees she says how good it is to have the car back!

Yesterday afternoon a party of us from Bonnie Oaks† went swimming in the slough, where you were. Of course they got bitten by snakes, and had to have medicine!

Last night we had supper with Mrs. Green at Bonnie Oaks, and she asked about you. Bless me if you didn't make quite an impression on everyone! Think of my sweet kitten-cat doing that, simply by being.

Last night, also, I had brief private talks with Chaunse and Tockie, first him and then her. It just happened to happen. And then, sort of fragmentary, came out something that rather surprised me. He and she are having difficulties between themselves. It is no wonder; but I was surprised. He is in a bad state, a state which makes it quite a task and a problem for her to, as the saying goes, live with him. I know he can be difficult, very. Unreasonable, vindictive, distempered, and all the rest. They have invited mother and myself to have dinner with them today at Marquette—where you were. After dinner, I hope to go into things with them, and see if I can isolate the main cause of the trouble—and then see what can be done about it. I feel it would be unfortunate if they broke up—yet, as I sense things now, they are surely heading for the rocks, unless something corresponding is done.

I've begun work, much as I said I would. Arranging, getting things in order, etc. With tonight, all outside doing will cease; and tomorrow morning I'll pitch in in earnest.

Let me know if Bertha had your dress sent to you. If not, I'll see about it. Your jacket is here. Do you want it sent, or shall I bring it when I come[?] It won't be any trouble to send it.

Yesterday a letter came from Fred Leighton, with the following—

> It was good to have met Marjorie that night at Mori's. I only regret that you had to leave so soon after my arrival in New York. Fritz Peters had a letter from Chicago the other day mentioning your arrival, a meeting, etc., and mentioning how much everyone liked Marjorie.

* wold

† Bonnie Oaks was the estate of Katharine "Tockie" Green, near which the Portage Experiment took place. She and fellow participant Charles Dupee eventually married.

The letter, of course, was from Maxine.* She, I gather, acts as the news agency for the wide flung members of what was once my Chicago world.

Eleanor Green is suddenly going to New York, leaving today. Driving with a friend.

Last night at the supper table Mother said to Mrs. Green that you had become a daughter of hers. She too is following the progress of your trip.

So you are staying over Sunday at the Hubbards? Good. A break in the trip. And rest, and a stretching. And tomorrow—Santa Fe!

Hope you will see—what's his name?—Kiker, the lawyer, just right away—and then let me know, also just right away, how things stand.

This I now note, is a full three-page letter, not without some gossip. And now realize that I was able to write it, only because she was just a sweet one.
Jean

By the way, I feel that Chaunse and Tockie ought to get out of Milwaukee—but about their going to New York I have reservations, which I'll tell you about when I get there. Meanwhile, I'm wondering if he could get any outside work to do in Colo or New Mexico. If I am to drive Georgia's car down, it may happen that I'll propose to Chaunse that he drive with me, returning by train a week after arriving in the Southwest. They have saved enough to make this possible, if it would really benefit him. In this case, he'd have the trip, a sort of vacation away from the spot in which he has been held down; and in Denver he'd see our old friend Bill Lowry—and there might be something for Chaunse at the airport. As I've mentioned, he is handy with his hands, and likes it. Unfortunately, he is specialized to do nothing outside of the business world—selling—and he hates this—and this is one seat of his trouble—a big one.

We've had plenty of rain here. Today is cold and overcast.

I still go to sleep with comparative ease. I still get up comparatively early. Yesterday morning I had breakfast at 8:30. This morning at 9:00. And this morning was Sunday. Tonight I'll go to bed early, and who knows—tomorrow I may get mother's breakfast for her an hour before she gets down!

* Maxine Mitchell was another member of Toomer's Chicago-based Gurdjieff group.

Marjorie Content to Jean Toomer
[Posted in Colorado Springs, Monday, June 11, 1934]
Sunday—June 10, 1934

My dear—my sweet. I wish you were here. We are lying out on a sunny slope of pasture—with pine trees behind and across on the other slope. not far from the log ranch houses—the corrals—the barns—the tepees. just having breakfasted heartily on fruit—cereal—eggs—muffins and coffee—home grown milk cream and butter—(with some buttermilk specially churned for Georgia because I told Ralph while fixing breakfast that I had been promising her some buttermilk) The birds are singing all around and the morning doves making that strange sound of theirs.

We had a wild day yesterday—It seems almost as if it couldn't have happened all in one day. I noticed after the motor warmed up. a strange and ominous noise. stopped at a garage and found that the bearing needed grease. We greased that and oiled other engine bearings—and then started out of town the wrong direction (2nd time) for 11 miles!—before we discovered it!—

We had decided to turn off route 30 at a place called Kearney and drop south to another road and later on further south to US 40 N.—from which I could hit the ranch directly instead of going way north to Denver and then coming 90 miles south to here—We sailed along south on a fine gravel road, noticing the ground was drenched and baking and cracking in the sun on the sides of the road—Suddenly there in front of us was a bridge—out—and down with the river running over it.—We went into a farmhouse and the woman of the house couldn't understand how we had come this far—It seems that the last two bridges we had crossed had been repaired in the half hour before we reached them. There was nothing to do but go back about 14 miles and take another more roundabout road south. Eventually we got down to where we wished—stopping again to grease the fan bearing which was acting up again worse than ever. By lunch-time the noise in there was awful (after the 2 greasings) and I thought it must be something else. Found a fair sized town called Norton. The mechanics all gathered around and looked mystified. Finally they decided to replace the water pump connection and grease the fan bearing with the heaviest and stickiest grease available—They did this while we lunched. and we have had no more trouble since then.

On thru Kansas + Colorado. Georgia just loving every inch of the road—sharing with me some of my pet remembered beauties—such as the way the tumbleweed piles against the fences—and the furrows of brown earth against the sky—and also disclosing through her eyes new beauties which had eluded me in the past—It was all very delightful—She kept saying—"Isn't it wonderful how I drop all that shaky and foolish sensation—Now I feel capable of anything. Isn't it awful that I'm going to just love it again!"—(with variations on the theme—this was her constantly recurring refrain)

I began to feel a bit pressed for time as I wanted to reach the ranch in daylight—I wasn't sure that I could find the road after dark—We were going along when we both suddenly espied a field of waving wheat and on its far side black railroad cars and a white silo—We both exclaimed at the wonder of it—when G. said: "That's a photograph"—I said "It surely is"—Said she—"Stop + do it!"—With that encouragement I backed up, unloaded all equipment and started work—A man drove over from his farmhouse to see if we were in trouble—and needed help—Other drivers stopped too—I took 3 different shots of it—and <u>promised</u> if any turned out well—that it should be called "Portrait of Georgia O'Keeffe"—

Which amused us both mightily—

Fully refreshed with this exciting experience—we again sped over Kansas and arrived (after a vile detour) at Limon—a small town near here (about 55 miles as a matter of fact) where we phoned Ralph to say we would be here—sent off telegrams to you and Stieglitz—filled up the gas tank—grabbed some sandwiches—It was then about 7:30 and the sun going down as we turned into the funny little back road to here—

We found indications of the right road until—after dark we came to a fork with no sign and both choices looking equally important or unimportant. While sitting considering I saw car lights behind—and when it approached blew my horn violently until he stopped. We then asked the road to Kiowa. He said, "Follow me"—and off he started—and led us a terrible chase thru the blackness, over bridges whose loose boards thundered under us—at 50 miles an hour. I clung to the wheel and concentrated on the road—and managed to keep his tail lights in sight most of the time. The road does this [here she illustrates three successive narrow, rolling hills, tall enough to hide the leading car from the following car's view] and at the top of each hill we felt as if we were dropping off into nothingness.

We had put the top down at sunset because everything was so beautiful—but while chasing the tail lights—a big storm came up—Lightning added its flashes to the drama—Clouds dropped rain all around us—but not where we were. In Kiowa we put up the top—Georgia straightened out her side unexpectedly and squashed my finger—However it wasn't painful for long and this morning is all OK—

<u>We actually found the ranch</u>—by 9:30. It was good to get here. Georgia went to bed at once and I went down to the campfire where Ralph was telling stories—where they were singing some Indian songs—

He has acquired a wife since I have been here—She seems quite nice—and the household better arranged—tho it's always pretty good, as he does most of the cooking—He seems happier + gayer too—and took to Georgia to from the first instant—I have a suspicion that she is going to wrangle a buffalo skull out of him before we leave—an object which she has long coveted—

At present there is a group of about 25 boys here—They are boy scouts who came up from La Junta a week ago, and leave today—*

I wish you could meet Ralph—Some things you would have in common—Some you would quarrel with him for—and on some you could very decidedly show him larger aspects—I feel that it would be very good—He is a man of character.

We are loafing here today—to give G. a chance to rest up—and to accustom to the altitude of about 5000 ft.—When I first suggested yesterday that we stay, she was for getting to Santa Fe tonight—but today she is delighted that we stayed. and shows signs of wanting to stay longer. However—I think the Santa Fe lure will win out by tomorrow morning—plus me.

She enunciated a strange doctrine yesterday—"The one thing people cannot stand is the truth!"—Does that seem to go with G.?—or do you think it refers to her present chaos?—I'll tackle her on it one of these days—

Of course I miss you—but even with you in Portage—it is very different from being alone. You are at once my base and my apex—Always there—Life is certainly a different thing—with this incorporation—

In spite of this—I would love a word from you—and I hope to find it in Santa Fe.—

After checking up I find we went 452 miles yesterday—How amazing! I did all the driving—just why I don't know.

Georgia has difficulty in finding things to write to Stieglitz! And here am I covering pages with nothings and only being too lazy to write all the things I have to say to you.

Some of them that have come up during the day don't recur to me when I start to write—I am quite out of the practice of writing too. I mean this kind of letter—where one really wants to communicate—

This is enough for one morning. What will your letters be like? Curiosity is strong—Well. I know they'll be fine and what's the real difference if it's one kind of fineness or another?—

How goes the work dear?

M.†

* The group of boy scouts from La Junta are the Koshare Dancers, a famous and still-vibrant Boy Scout troop that performs Indian dances throughout the nation and maintains a museum of Indian artifacts and scout-made replicas.

Marjorie Content to Jean Toomer
Telegram from Colorado Springs, CO
Monday, June 11, 1934, 11:40 a.m.
JEAN TOOMER
PORTAGE WIS
GEORGIA DELIGHTED IF SOMEONE CAN BRING CAR OUT TO HER STOP IF DONE SHE MUST SEND OWNERS CARD TO RUSSELL AND WIRE INSTRUCTIONS TO MARGARET LET US KNOW SANTAFE DELIGHTFUL DAY AT RANCH WORLD RIDERS RIDING HIGH WITH EARTH BEING AS STIMULANT LOVE
NO SIG*

Jean Toomer to Marjorie Content
Portage, WI
Monday, June 11, 1934

And so! Shelton, Neb. The second day! 420 miles!

What kids you are, yea, great kids, world-riders! Tough girls with a streak of beauty!

Everyone here, everyone there, seems agreed that you and I do "hit it off" pretty well. Georgia, too. So, good.

And the flask. I was wondering about that. And about the Johnnie Walker too.

Here too there has been rain, and thunder and lightning, and a minor cloud burst. You . . . you really were on the high seas, weren't you; and you were good officers of the ship, you brought her through.

While I was having the midday meal, your wire from Colorado Springs came. By the way, you may as well, in fact you'd better sign the telegrams. They come with the "Unsigned" so prominent that it's no use. Besides, now there's no reason for the "secrecy." The whole town knows you were here; and they know, or think they know, many other things besides. So sign your own name, or initials.

Remember me saying in New York that I had some psychological work to do here, preparing mother for my absence, for my trips and stays away, etc. Well, the needed "preparing" was done while you were here that weekend. Now mother accepts everything. She no longer inwardly holds me, but has a feeling that everything is all right. She knows it is a new world and a new life I have, with you—and she feels <u>in</u> it—so that's that.

Glad you had such a fine day at the ranch. And reading Earth-Being![*] Already! What energy and vitality you have!

I'm going to phone Russell around 5 this afternoon. And then wire you at Santa Fe. The last I heard, he wants to leave for the east tomorrow, Tuesday. This won't give time for Georgia to get the owner's card to him at Barrington. She'd best send it, I think, to him at Lake George. But I'll put all of this definitely in my wire, after I talk to him. Just now it occurs to me that he may not know the car is in Lake George, but may think it is in New York. What difference, if any, this will make, I can't tell. We'll see. And you'll get a wire, perhaps a night letter, tomorrow morning.

Today, for the first time since leaving NY, I'm sending my laundry out. Quite a bundle! Yesterday I wore my fawn pants, to break them in—and got a spot of car grease on them. Grief! But it will come out.

All morning I worked. All afternoon I will work. At first I had a bit of resistance to this "settling down," as something in me wants to be moving; but I soon overcame it, and did things.

After dinner yesterday I had a long talk with Chaunse and Tockie, too complicated to write about here. During it, I tentatively proposed that, if I drive Georgia's car out to the Southwest, Chaunse accompany me. I said I couldn't be sure, as yet. It was simply a possibility that I wanted to mention. Both he and Tockie thought it would be an excellent thing.

The girl is coming to get some typing to do tonight. I do think I will be finished with the unwieldy part of the job in three weeks, more or less.

Now I'm anxious to know what you have found out about "business" down there.

and much love to the skipper of the good ship—and Georgia seems all ready for the kind of vital life I wish for her—and so, to you both—holé, holé!

Jean

Even Chaunse, that erstwhile 100 percent American who shied at all "foreign" influences, now says "HOLÉ" with great gusto!

And now to confess something. Now that I've stopped drinking hard licker, I have a yen for sweets. What these topers[†] won't do! Believe me, when I go downtown I'm going to buy a box of candy!

* *Earth-Being* was an autobiography Toomer worked on in 1930. Jean Toomer Papers 12.371–87.

† drunks or scoundrels

Marjorie Content to Jean Toomer
Taos, NM
Tuesday, June 12, 1934

Jean dear—

We pulled in here last night about 9 o'clock—Georgia and Ralph became so chummy over skulls that G. walked off—not with one—but with 4 or 5—of varying shapes and sizes—so we didn't get away from there til about 11a.m..—Somehow it was a hard drive—the car very balky until I found a gallon of kerosene—and still not very peppy on rough grades. Then too—there was so much to look at and enjoy that we were both very tired.

Came to El Chamiso* and after baths felt much better—my ears are rather buzzy and my head either light or heavy—I'm not sure which—but not really normal—

Judge Kiker seems elusive—With an office at Raton—another in Santa Fe—and a home and family here. he is at none of them—but off at court somewhere else—He is expected at one or all of these places momentarily—I have written duplicate letters in the hope of catching him somewhere soon—

Meanwhile—we have seen two houses—and in the course of a visit to Taos Plaza—everybody in town!! We are to see another house this afternoon—maybe—We will decide on none until we have been down to Alcalde (Marie Garland's†) which G. has a certain fondness for—and looked over the situation there—

We are going to start off tomorrow morning—stop there—go on down to Santa Fe—get mail—have another shot at Kiker and come back here—collect baggage and move in somewhere—

G. + I decided that I drove to Chicago with a friend—nobody in particular—just a friend—The buzzing if any, will thereby be postponed for a while.—

I find this place different now—Of course—what I mean is that I must be changed—I actually haven't even been to the pueblo—I have on a white dress—and am looking for a house—A house big enough to house someone over 6 ft.—A house comfortable enough for someone who values those matters rather higher than I do.—or should I say—has a different idea of comfort? And even his being there is not so certain—It must be fixed so that it is an elastic house—perhaps just for Georgia alone—perhaps for 3 or 4 people—Well—it must and shall be done—and tomorrow if possible—!—

* The El Chamiso Lodge in Taos, later called the Sagebrush Inn, where O'Keeffe painted in the summer of 1931.

† O'Keeffe's friend Marie Garland was a famed hostess and a guest-ranch owner. O'Keeffe lived at her H & M Ranch and painted in the area in the summers of 1929–1931. Robinson, *Georgia O'Keeffe*, 359–60.

Mail—mail—That's what I want—well. That must wait until tomorrow too—There was too much to do here today and we were both a bit woozy—

Just as I had visualized your meeting me in Denver, there arises the possibility of your driving Georgia's car out, and I have to construct a new picture with vague outlines as yet.

I could write more but have letters to get in the mail before the P. O. closes and so will cut short.—

All goes well with us——but I can't seem to think about work—or to even look really at anything—I am just a businesswoman—who must attend to certain matters—

I drive around with blind eyes—focused only on business matters and a sort of impossible or improbable house—

Wrote Mother Latimer the other day—just like that—

Only about three weeks to go—then home again—

M.*

To Jean Toomer
Telegram from Santa Fe, NM
Wednesday, June 13, 1934, 2:43 p.m.

JEAN TOOMER
PORTAGE WIS
MAIL FOR MARJORIE CONTENT UNCALLED FOR STOP HAVE HOLD ORDER FROM HER DATED JUNE FIRST ADVISING SHE HAD BEEN DELAYED ENROUTE
STEVENSON ASSISTANT POSTMASTER

Jean Toomer to Marjorie Content
Note for Telegram from Portage, WI
Wednesday, June 13, 1934, 8:22 p.m.

Marjorie Content,
Wires have been hot to locate you and but for Spud† I don't know what I might have done stop you mustn't disappear like that stop answer at once
Signed, Jean

† Spud Johnson was a writer, a critic, and a fixture in the Taos artist colony. He was secretary to Mabel Dodge Luhan and published the little magazine *Laughing Horse*.

Marjorie Content to Jean Toomer
Telegram from Santa Fe, NM
Thursday, June 14, 1934, 8:47 a.m.
JEAN TOOMER
PORTAGE WIS
LETTER AND TELEGRAM RECIEVED MOVING TOMORROW INTO NICE HOUSE THIRTY FIVE MILES FROM HERE ON WAY TO TAOS STOP MAILING ADRESS THERE ESPANOLA TELEGRAM IN CARE OF GARLAND AT ALCALDE BUSINESS MAN OUT OF TOWN UNTIL FRIDAY STOP GOING TO TAOS NOW FOR BAGGAGE GREETINGS FROM US BOTH
MARJORIE*

Jean Toomer to Marjorie Content
Portage, WI
Friday, June 15, 1934

You dear tired woozy darling!
Yes, but she was just a Navigating Officer! She was just the skipper of a great ship! She brought the ship into port!

Your letter from Taos, just arrived, moved me to write the above.

No wonder you didn't wire me at once, being so tired and having all those things to do, all at once and quickly. But, my dear, that was one reason why I worried when I didn't hear. I sort of knew the condition you'd be in, during the last stages. However, that's over—and you are probably rested by now. I hope so.

I wondered how you'd feel the Southwest this time. I knew you'd feel it differently. You almost had to. Because you are different, with other needs and desires and aims.

I'm very glad your hunt for a suitable house (with all the various requirements!) was successful so soon. Very.

Of course try to get the "business" moving and settled as soon as possible; but, on the other hand, don't let unavoidable delays fret you. Do what you can—and then "take it easy." I had already figured on the possibility of delays. Sometimes they can't be helped, sometimes just when one most wants quick clean action. Do the best you can—and let happen what must happen. In whatever time must be taken. All I need to know is precisely what the facts and conditions are. Then I can act. And, whatever the said facts and conditions, we won't let them interfere with the flowing of our lives this summer—or ever. Always we will live—and, when necessary, let the facts catch up with us.

[. . .]*

Yesterday Mother told me how much she liked your "New York Interior." This is the second time she has mentioned it.

There seemed to be a sadness in your letter that made me want to reach you at once, be with you, tell you again and again that you mustn't and oughtn't and shouldn't be away from me, even for business, and give my sweet bunny such a rousing hug that she'd feel very very happy at once, and hold her for a long time, so that the happiness wouldn't leave her, ever.

Last night after supper I took Mother for a drive up US 51 round Endeavor—one of the few roads you weren't on. We drifted along at an easy 30-mile pace—the way she likes to go, so as to take in the fields, the condition of the crops, and everything. As the sun set and dusk came on, I thought of you and Georgia way down far off in Española, having your first evening in the house, your first night in its beds—perhaps getting supper and then talking a short while and then going to bed early, feeling that the long trip and search for quarters was over at last. I wanted to be with you. I asked myself why in god's name I was up here, with you there. Or why you weren't here too. In any case, why we left each other a week ago, why we weren't together, wherever it might be. In addition to my understandable human feelings about you going off, I have, I've found, curious deep male feelings about my woman going off out of my immediate world. These feelings were doubtless at the base of my concern when I didn't get a wire from you Monday night.

And today—this is your first day in the new house, the house that I imagine but cannot see. It is about eleven o'clock there, perhaps too early for you to be getting lunch. I wonder what you see when you look inside the house. I wonder what you see when you look outside—other similar houses?—mountains?—the valley?—the river? And do you see me in it, and wonder how I will like it, and for how long?

That country is surely my country too. I have a love for it. Yet, as you know, I hate it also. I don't know all the reasons why I hate it. It is almost as if, ages ago, long ages ago, I suffered deeply in it—and a memory of that suffering sometimes stirs in the regions of myself far below consciousness. I want to found and build a world there. Also I feel that no good can come of it to me or to anyone I love. I feel it is magnificent and challenging. I feel it is hostile, like a great enemy, like a God who is trying to do me down. But these are feelings born of the past. I can't rid myself of them; but, on the other hand, I know it will be different with you there, and I feel I am coming to a new world.

love

Jean

* A paragraph, here omitted, concerns the details of Toomer bringing O'Keeffe's car to New Mexico.

Jean Toomer to Marjorie Content
Cedar Rapids, IA
Handwritten on Hotel Roosevelt stationery
Sunday, July 1, 1934, 9:00 p.m.

Darling!
Surprised you! Yes, here I am, on my way—at just the town where you made your first stop, after leaving Barrington and then Geneva at just the time you did, 3:00 p.m.!!!!! I got here at 7:30—and sent you a wire.

It happened to work out so that I got away from the Chicago region today.

Chaunse and I stayed with the Walcotts last night—and had a fine time. Then, this morning, we left the little gascar at Barrington while we drove into Chicago in the Ford. Saw the baby and Max and Shirley—stayed there about half an hour—then started back to Barrington.* On Michigan Ave I stopped at a Haylers store where they had a sale of Johnny Walker. But—grief—they couldn't sell any liquor on Sunday until after 1:00 p.m. I couldn't wait. The Walcotts were expecting us to lunch at 1:00. So back to Barrington we literally flew. Yes, Russell's name, Samuel Peppy, is a good one for this car.

Then, right after lunch, we began packing and getting ready. Chaunse was scheduled to be back in Portage by 6:00 so as to drive back to Milwaukee with Tockie. And I—well, I just simply couldn't keep myself from moving. Besides, all of them had worked up a fine send-off for me. It was the psychological moment for my departure—so off I went, Chaunse driving the little car just in front of me until we reached Algonquin—and then, a parting of the ways, he going north to McHenry and Madison and Portage, and I going south [to] Geneva and US 30—and here I am!

My O my, did they—Russ, Eugenia, and Chaunse—kid me! Did they!! They began last night at supper—and today they fastened a cupid on the car's radiator to act as a ship's figurehead!! Yes sir, they have it—and with much proof—that I'm just crazy about you, and that you are just the same way about me—and, bless me, they knew I liked the razzing!!! Never before have they had the opportunity. They certainly made good of it—and we all had just lots of fun.

Russ + Eugenia have in mind the Southwest during Sept. In Sept. they may come down. I think driving G's car to Barrington took the edge off Russ's urgency to set off anywhere at once. Maybe later.

Father Latimer had a bad night last night. I phoned Mother to find out how he was.

* Max and Shirley Grove were friends from Chicago Gurdjieff circles who were serving as foster parents for Jean Toomer and Margery Latimer's now nearly two-year-old daughter Margery.

Chaunse is going to wire me about what he finds on his return. He'll send the wire here to Cedar Rapids, as I was pretty sure I'd be here tonight.

And maybe I'll get a wire from you? I did pick up one at Max's this morning

Tomorrow morning I get up early—6:30. I plan to make Gothenburg tomorrow night—and—the camp Tuesday evening!!!!

So now for a bath and to bed!

But not without a sweet kiss for my S.O. S.B. B.G.!!

and love
Jean

(over)

As I crossed the great Mississippi I recited—almost chanted—that part of "The Blue Meridian" which has to do with the great brown river. My emotions just suddenly remembered it. I felt I was engaged in a sacred ritual, in a prayer, in a song of triumph!

> The Mississippi, sister of the Ganges,
> Main artery of earth in the western world,
> Is waiting to become
> In the spirit of America
> A sacred river,
> Whoever lifts that river
> Lifts himself and all America,
> Whoever lifts himself
> Makes that great brown river smile;
> The blood of earth and the blood of man
> Course swifter and rejoice when we spiritualize.

Bibliography

Austin, Mary. "Cults of the Pueblos: An Interpretation of Some Native Ceremonials." *Century* 109 (Nov. 1924): 28–35.

Burke, Flannery. *From Greenwich Village to Taos.* Lawrence: University Press of Kansas, 2008.

Byrd, Rudolph P. *Jean Toomer's Years with Gurdjieff: Portrait of an Artist, 1923–1936.* Athens: University of Georgia Press, 1990.

Byrd, Rudolph P., and Henry Louis Gates Jr. "Jean Toomer's Racial Self-Identification." In *Cane*, edited by Rudolph Byrd and Henry Louis Gates Jr., lxvi–lxx. New York: Norton, 2011.

———. "'Song of the Son': The Emergence and Passing of Jean Toomer." In *Cane*, edited by Rudolph Byrd and Henry Louis Gates Jr., xix–lxvi. New York: Norton, 2011.

Content, Marjorie. Letters and Telegrams to Jean Toomer, June 8, 9, 11, 12, 14, and 16, 1934. Jean Toomer Papers, Box 8, Folders 251–53, James Weldon Johnson Collection, Beinecke Rare Book and Manuscript Library, New Haven, CT. Copyright Estate of Marjorie Content.

Dekker, Carolyn. "Jean Toomer, Sojourner: Striking Experience in the South and Southwest." *MELUS* 39 no.4 (2014): 92–113.

Deloria, Philip J. *Playing Indian.* New Haven, CT: Yale University Press, 1998.

Diffendal, Robert F., Duane R. Mohlman, Richard G. Corner, F. Edwin Harvey, K. J. Warren, Scott Summerside, Roger K. Pabian, and Duane A. Eversoll. "Field Guide to the Geology of the Harlan County Lake Area, Harlan County, Nebraska—with a History of Events Leading to Construction of Harlan County Dam." *Papers in Natural Resources* (2002): 77.

Gordon-McCutchan, R. C. *The Taos Indians and the Battle for Blue Lake*. Santa Fe, NM: Red Crane Books, 1991.

Harrington, J. P. "Old Indian Geographical Names Around Santa Fe, New Mexico." *American Anthropologist* 22, no. 4 (1920): 341–59.

Hubbard, Ralph. *American Indian Crafts*. New York: Plume Trading and Sales, 1935.

Kerman, Cynthia Earl, and Richard Eldridge. *The Lives of Jean Toomer: A Hunger for Wholeness*. Baton Rouge: Louisiana State University Press, 1987.

Luhan, Mabel Dodge. *Winter in Taos*. Taos, NM: La Palomas de Taos, 1987.

Lutenski, Emily. "'A Small Man in Big Spaces': The New Negro, the Mestizo, and Jean Toomer's Southwestern Writing." *MELUS* 33, no. 1 (Spring 2008): 11–32.

Porter, Katherine Anne. *The Never-Ending Wrong*. Boston, MA: Little, Brown, 1977.

Redman, Tim. "C. H. Douglas and Social Credit." In *Ezra Pound and Italian Fascism*, 51–75. New York: Cambridge University Press, 1991.

"Register of the Atwood, Ormsby, and Green family papers, 1853–1998." Finding Aid at Wisconsin Historical Society, Madison, WI. http://digital.library.wisc.edu/1711.dl/wiarchives.uw-whs-mss00989 (accessed July 12, 2015).

Reily, Nancy Hopkins. *Georgia O'Keeffe, A Private Friendship, Part 1: Walking the Sun Prairie Land*. Santa Fe, NM: Sunstone Press, 2011.

Ridge, Lola. Letter to David Lawson, May 1935. Lola Ridge Papers, Sofia Smith Collection, Smith College, Northampton, MA.

———. Letter to Marjorie Content, June 18, 1935. Marjorie Content Papers and Photographs, Box 1. Yale Collection of American Literature, Beinecke Rare Book and Manuscript Library, New Haven, CT.

Robinson, Roxana. *Georgia O'Keeffe: A Life*. Hanover, NH: University Press of New England, 1989.

Rolland, Romain. *Letters of Romain Rolland and Malwida von Meysenbug 1890–1891*. Translated by Thomas J. Wilson. New York: Henry Holt, 1933.

Rothman, Hal. *Devil's Bargains: Tourism in the Twentieth Century American West*. Lawrence: University Press of Kansas, 2000.

Rudnick, Lois Palken. *Utopian Vistas: The Mabel Dodge Luhan House and the American Counterculture*. Albuquerque: University of New Mexico Press, 1996.

Scruggs, Charles. "Jean Toomer: Fugitive." *American Literature* 47, no. 1 (Mar. 1975): 84–96.

Stasi, Paul. "A 'Synchronous but More Subtle Migration': Passing and Primitivism in Toomer's *Cane*." *Twentieth-Century Literature* 55, no. 2 (Summer 2009): 145–74.

Tobin, Daniel. "Modernism, Leftism, and the Spirit: The Poetry of Lola Ridge." In *Light in Hand: Selected Early Poems of Lola Ridge*. Niantic, CT: Quale Press, 2007.

Toomer, Jean. *A Drama of the Southwest*, holograph draft, n.d. Jean Toomer Papers, Box 44, Folders 914–16. Yale University Library, Beinecke Rare Book and Manuscript Library, James Weldon Johnson Collection, New Haven, CT.

———. *A Drama of the Southwest*, notes, n.d. Jean Toomer Papers, Box 44, Folder 913. Yale University Library, Beinecke Rare Book and Manuscript Library, James Weldon Johnson Collection, New Haven, CT.

———. *A Drama of the Southwest*, typescript, n.d. Jean Toomer Papers, Box 44, Folder 917. Yale University Library, Beinecke Rare Book and Manuscript Library, James Weldon Johnson Collection, New Haven, CT.

———. *Earth-Being*, n.d. and 1930. Jean Toomer Papers, Box 12, Folders 371–87.

———. New Mexico Notebook, n.d. Jean Toomer Papers, Box 65, Folder 1482.

———. Letters to Marjorie Content, June 7, 10, 13, 14, and 19, 1934. Jean Toomer Papers, Box 8, Folders 251–254. Yale University Library, Beinecke Rare Book and Manuscript Library, James Weldon Johnson Collection, New Haven, CT.

———. "Blue Meridian." In *The New Caravan*, edited by Alfred Kreymborg, Lewis Mumford, and Paul Rosenfeld, 633–53. New York: Norton, 1936.

———. "The Experience." In *A Jean Toomer Reader*, edited by Frederik L. Rusch, 33–76. New York: Oxford University Press, 1993.

———. "A New Race in America." In *A Jean Toomer Reader*, edited by Frederik L. Rusch, 105. New York: Oxford University Press, 1993.

———. *Cane*. In *Cane*, edited by Rudolph P. Byrd and Henry Louis Gates Jr., 1–119. New York: Norton, 2011.

Turner, Darwin T. "The Failure of a Playwright." *CLA Journal* 10 (June 1967): 308–18.

———. "Jean Toomer Exile." In *In a Minor Chord: Three African American Writers and Their Search for Identity*, 1–59. Carbondale: Southern Illinois University Press, 1971.

———. Introduction to *Cane*, by Jean Toomer, ix–xxv. New York: Boni & Liveright, 1975.

Waters, Frank. *To Possess the Land: A Biography of Arthur Rochford Manby*. Chicago, IL: Swallow Press, 1973.

Zigrosser, Carl. "Gurdjieff." *New Republic* 59, no. 757 (June 5, 1929): 66–69.

Index

www.ingramcontent.com/pod-product-compliance
Ingram Content Group UK Ltd.
Pitfield, Milton Keynes, MK11 3LW, UK
UKHW031026021026
476215UK00001B/23

9 780826 370440